SISTER ANSELMA SCOLLARD OSB is a Benedictine contemplative nun of St Cecilia's Abbey, Ryde, Isle of Wight. She has a double degree in philosophy and sculpture from the University of California. She also has an MA in philosophy from the University of Warwick, with a special interest in aesthetics. Before entering St Cecilia's, she held a senior lectureship in sculpture, during which time she travelled extensively in Italy studying the history of the art of the *Quattrocentro* and Renaissance periods, and in France, where her particular interest was in the sculpture and bas reliefs of early medieval cathedrals and churches; during this period, she took a *Certificat d'études françaises*. At St Cecilia's, her practical work in sculpture has evolved into an interest in architectural landscape, the making and designing of furniture and various garden structures, and to ornamental trees and their situation in a monastic setting. She continues to write on aesthetic matters and the connection between art and religion.

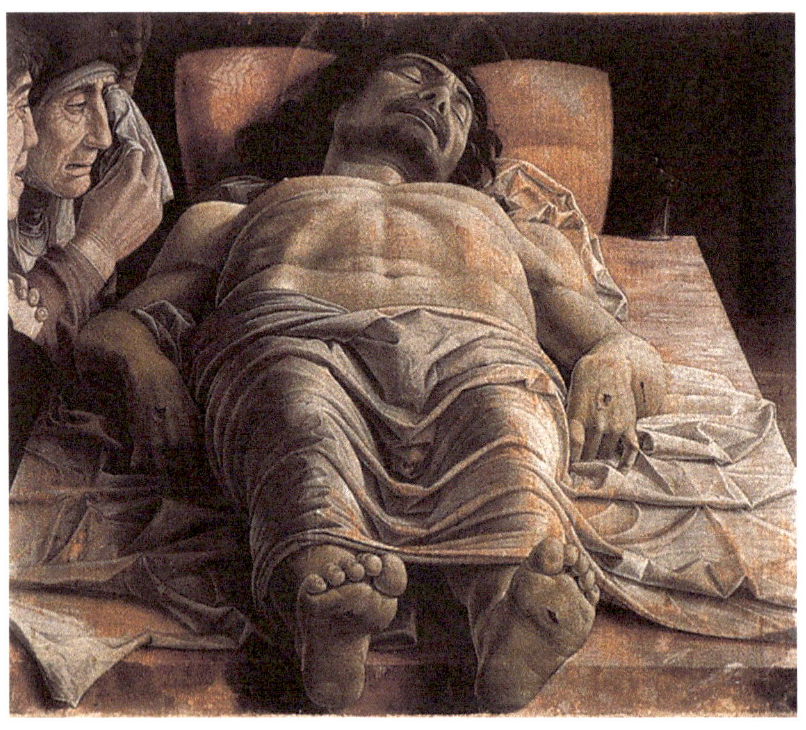

'Presenting death in its finality' (p.67). *Lamentation of Christ (Il Cristo Morto)*, Andrea Mantegna. Image credit: Wikicommons

Art, Truth & Time

Essays in Art

Sr Anselma Scollard OSB

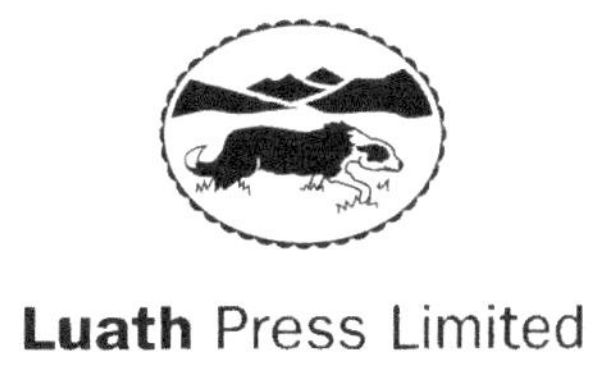

Luath Press Limited

EDINBURGH

www.luath.co.uk

First Published 2019

ISBN: 978-1-912147-53-3

The paper used in this book is recyclable. It is made from low chlorine pulps produced in a low energy, low emission manner from renewable forests.

Printed and bound by CPI Antony Rowe, Chippenham

Typeset in 10.5 point Sabon by Lapiz

Ninianae Abbatissae

Matri Amantissimae

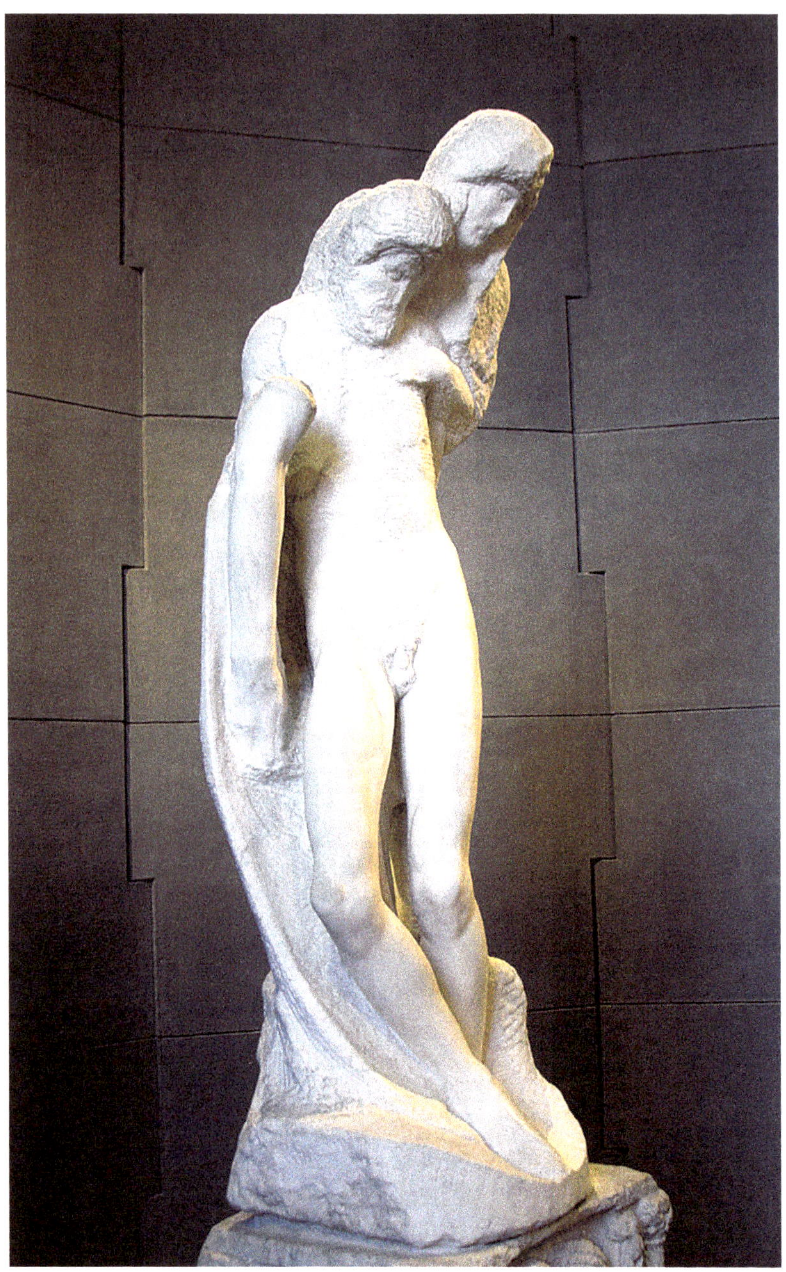

'The last work of an extraordinarily prolific career, it is Michelangelo's final statement' (p.71). *The Rondanini Pietà*, Michelangelo. Image credit: Wikicommons

Contents

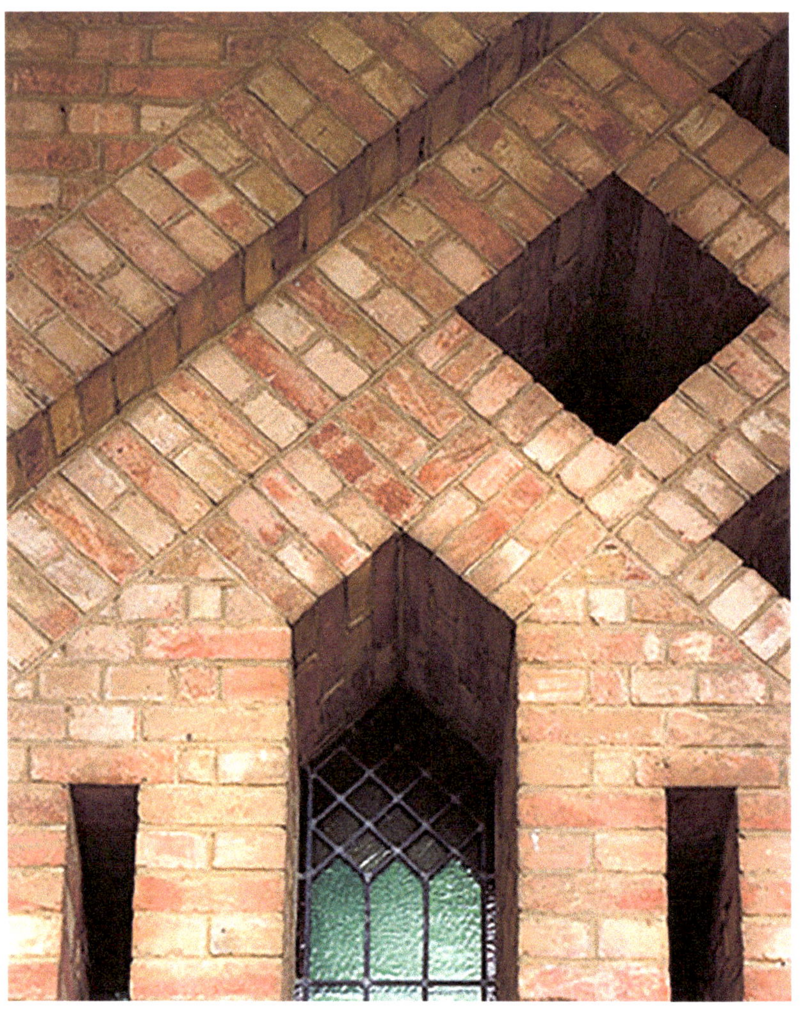

'Beauty is founded on the perfection of a thing, where measure and order are of the first importance' Dom Paul Bellot (p.88). Dom Bellot window, Quarr Abbey

Acknowledgements

MY PARENTS, Rosalind Thomas, Albert Hofstadter, Ettore and Marisa Pattofatto, Roy Oxlade and Rose Wylie, Luigi Canale, the Abbess and Community of St Cecilia's Abbey, Richard Demarco, who has always given me his support, Gavin MacDougall, who has kindly agreed to publish this book, and Alice Latchford, who has been so helpful in the editing of the book.

Foreword

SISTER ANSELMA SCOLLARD'S book of essays, with its thought-provoking title *Art, Truth & Time*, should help act as an antidote to the problems now besetting the world of the arts, just as the arts are thus considered a healing balm to suffering humanity. The arts in general are subject to the malformation of truth in our distinctly materialistic society. Sr Anselma Scollard is well aware of this fast-developing problem. Ever since I first read her essays, I knew that I could rely on her profound understanding of the nature and purpose of art from her daily experience of her life as a member of an enclosed order of Benedictine nuns as well as someone educated as an artist. She is commitmented to a life of prayer in the Benedictine Abbey of St Cecilia on the Isle of Wight, one of the places of religious pilgrimage in Europe where the sound of prayer can still be heard. I associate every Benedictine abbey with the beauty of its location in harmony with nature.

Sr Anselma's work elucidates my personal commitment to helping artists make proper use of art language which, according to Joseph Beuys, is our birthright in support of his firm belief that 'everyone is an artist'. By that, he insisted that everyone is born to be creative. He personified the true spirit of post-war contemporary art and he was therefore fully aware of the Celtic dimension in the process of the Christianisation of Europe emanating from the Hebridean sacred island of Iona, defining the monastic world of St Columba and his fellow missionaries. I would ask anyone reading these essays to relate them to The Demarco Archive (www.demarco-archive.ac.uk) as a large-scale collaborative work of art, as a veritable 'Gesamtkunstwerk', which came into being in the post-Second World War years, interlocked with the history of the Edinburgh Festival. These essays are essential reading for me in the immediate development of the Archive as a work of art and will surely help clarify the nature and purpose it as an academic resource; a resource inspired by our European cultural heritage in the second decade of the Third Millennium, expressing the passing of time within the Christian Era upon this planet which is defined poetically by Hugh MacDiarmid as a 'Bonnie Broukit Bairn' or a 'beautiful, neglected urchin'.

These essays defend the nature of art in its most exalted form, so that art is seen clearly ascending to the condition of prayer, enabling us to express our gratitude for the gift of life. It is a multi-faceted expression of our human capacity to love. It helps us heal the self-inflicted pain and sorrow resulting from human conflict. In a future continuing to be dominated by the uncontrollable growth of commercialised culture, mass media, the banking system (which continues to make the rich richer and the poor poorer) and the manufacturing of weapons of war, the very title of Sr Anselma's collection of essays instils in me a sense of hope in a world which can believe in the poetic words of John Keats – that 'Truth is Beauty and Beauty is Truth'.

Her preface to her essays is best defined in her own words. In these few words, she makes it clear that her essays are simply 'what art is about and how it expresses truth'. In short, studying Sister Anselma's essays has provided me with hope for the future of an art world much in need of her understanding of art language.

Richard Demarco

Kingston University Emeritus Professor
of European Cultural Studies

Preface

THE ESSAYS CONTAINED in this book were written over a fairly long period of time and served different purposes. Many were written as a philosophical or aesthetic critique of a then contemporary artist or exhibition. Others were written in a monastic context and for a monastic readership, others treat of contemporary, still endemic, attitudes about the nature of truth, its relation to religious belief and its effect on artistic creation. In these various contexts the views which I express form a gradual development in belief concerning what art is about and how it expresses truth. The 'problems' concerning present day art are based on a world view (specifically Western) which denies the significance of the cooperation between body and soul. In contemporary thought what was once the soul, has become mind or intellect – a conceptual process – which is considered as something separate and superior to the body; while the body is but a series of needs and functions which must be fulfilled. In this sense the body is inferior to the soul, and it (the body) has become the servant of the soul, rather than its helpmate. Artistic creation depends as much upon body as soul and the soul's intelligent use of the body's own way of understanding.

When there is a complete disjunction between body and soul, certain ideas come into being which recognise only one or the other of these two 'presences' and so emphasise one whilst excluding the other. Conceptual Art is such a phenomenon, where matter is no longer involved and there need be no material manifestation in the artistic 'object'. In a sense, there is no object, just a subject. Another example of the separation of body and soul is the absolute glorification of body, its desires and appetites to the complete disregard of the spirit. Jackson Pollock's 'Action Painting' might be an example of this. When there is this unnatural separation of body and soul, which comes as a result of the disregard of the intrinsic unity between the two the result is a world view which denies the existence of a Creator who has (with love) established an order in the universe whose highest manifestation is that of man, made of body and soul. Man has been entrusted with the guarding and protecting of this natural order through a respect for the gifts of imagination and understanding as much as a respect for the human intellect and its capacities.

Finally, there is the religious context within which these essays were written, giving them, I hope a particular clarity. All the essays were written since I entered the monastery, and each was preceded by prayer.

PART ONE

Art and Truth

The Experience of Truth

THE NOTION OF TRUTH, a belief that something exists, is real and can be found or at least experienced, has a comforting quality about it, a stability which underlies what we think and what we do. Even if we deny the existence of truth or think we have no access to it, everything we do and say as rational creatures refers to it even if only implicitly. It is symptomatic of our age that either it is said we cannot know it or, if it can be known, it must be limited to a scientific expression, that the only truth we can be sure about is revealed by the scientific method; it is analytic and deductive; any statements about reality which go beyond scientific principles are uncertain.

The biblical notion of truth, both in the Semitic and Greek sense, indicates something far richer and more comprehensive than the parameters set up by scientific method. Truth in the Old Testament is seen as a virtue. It implies value and is often coupled with the virtue of mercy *'hesed'*, a characteristic of the heart. Truth in this setting is usually translated as fidelity – a willed stability, duration, solidity of purpose, an enduring reality. None of these latter characteristics could be said to define contemporary society. It is not strange then that truth itself should be given such a limited definition, since those characteristics which have defined it in the past are found in little favour today. The Greek word for truth – *'aletheia'* – suggests something without veil: something literally unconcealed, something which is revealed. The clarity implied in this term, as with the Old Testament word *'emeth'*, can have a moral overtone. It can signify sincerity and uprightness, also completeness, totality, perfection – fullness. Thus, the two biblical expressions of truth, Semitic and

Greek, could be said to converge: truth is something which endures and is singular. It is pure in so far as it is not ambiguous or confused.

But truth is not just a reality which exists outside of us, which is what its scientific expression would have us believe. It, or the understanding of it, implies an attitude; it implies a belief – a certainty, not a restrictive certainty, which is dictated from without by a system, but an inner certainty. Truth and our attitude towards it, may be conscious or unconscious, but either way it grants assurance and confidence. In this sense truth approaches the traditional definition of faith – '*cum assensione cogitare*', to think with assent. The awareness of truth cannot be had by applying a method, as if it were the result of the application of some scientific equation. It exists whether we allude to it or not. For even if we apply a method to find out whether something is true, there must always be an underpinning of confidence. Our very ability to apply a method implies a true state of affairs, or a constancy which indicates that using this method will render a true answer. Truth necessarily manifests itself in specific instances, but the rules for its application must lie beyond the individual instances. To limit truth to the scientifically verifiable is to betray its ontological character – it is to betray reality. To say truth has an ontological character is substantial, that a statement can be found worthy of verification, either that it is verifiable by reference to some real object or state of affairs. To say that we experience a truth is to know something with certitude, even if this certitude does not render itself capable of a complete explanation. Here truth approaches faith, not necessarily by having as its object something with religious content, but by being accepted. This sense of truth will not exclude doubt, but by an assurance which is more than feeling and as something which is a lived attitude pervading one's actions and decisions, it will develop, in time, a stability which eschews the vagaries and uncertainties of relativism establishing a hope which does not deceive.

Art, Truth and Time

THE FOLLOWING IS MEANT to give some idea of how truth is reflected in an object of art and how this truth functions in relation to time: whether time determines the meaning of an artistic statement of truth, or whether that statement describes a reality which, although located in time, has horizons which extend beyond the immediate.

In what sense can art be about the truth, when truth is usually conceived of as the product of the discursive intellect, a description of a verifiable reality using concepts with fixed and specific meanings? In order to understand how truth can pertain to art, it is first necessary to see that truth is not limited to the intellect. Truth exists beyond and before the conceptual giving of meaning. An inability to map out by analytical reasoning the logic of certain meanings does not render them less significant and true. In a work of art meaning operates, is conveyed, differently. Reality can be described variously and is not for that less true. As Ernst Cassirer noted, the nature of reality is far richer than that which can be described by scientific concepts and formulae. To think that the truth of reality can be explained by discursive reasoning alone is an illusion. The work of art manifestly tells us this: 'For the aspects of things are innumerable, and they vary from moment to moment.'[1]

The truth spoken of in an object of art is contained within a framework – an artistically meaningful statement made up of related terms. These terms are not conceptual but intuitively perceived. They are variously: colour, surface, line, mass etc contained in and making

---

[1] Ernst Cassirer, *Language and Myth*.

up a whole. The logical confines of the artistic object are determined by the object and contained within it. The truth sustained within the object is the sum result of the fitness and necessity of its elements. This framework is established by the artist – be it a canvas edge or, for example, Brancusi's *Table of Silence*. The framework is one with the elements it contains. The meaning is to be found here within this space, and not explained by something outside it. It is understood as it presents itself.

Essentially what marks out the art object in its traditional sense (a tradition which has infinite horizons) from many objects, collections of objects, or phenomena on the artistic contemporary scene, is this sense of 'internal relatedness' which does not require something extraneous to it in order to be appreciated and understood. It needs no further verbal interpretation. It is basically self-sufficient.[2] This 'internal relatedness' which has been the *sine qua non* of the aesthetic entity until fairly recently has been abandoned in favour of an artistic freedom which makes no demands on the artist nor on his/her public; seeking, as it does, a value-free, meaning-free expression, whose interpretation or quality is determined by its contemporaneity. What we have at present then is a situation where meaning and significance no longer persist through time, but are decided by it. There is no internal necessity in the work, which makes it self-explanatory; rather the internal necessity is in the artist's need to speak about him/herself. There is nothing to be understood or perceived; we are no longer being presented with an ontological reality, but rather a sociological or psychological phenomenon, which does not present itself so much to our aesthetic understanding as to our psyche; there is not a meaning to be grasped but an experience to be had. This *passagère* reality demands nothing, and gives nothing. It neither sustains nor enriches.

---

[2] Louis Dupre, *Symbols of the Sacred*. p.72.

The fact that this form of art depends on time and its proximity to the changing moment for its meaning in no way guarantees that sameness and boredom will be avoided. A work of art which is the genuine result of a living and creative intuition must necessarily move beyond the present moment and, whilst the truth it enunciates will strike a chord of familiarity yet it will not be fixed by it. Aesthetic truth, aesthetic excellence, is an entirely free enterprise; it is not subject to time, it moves, it endures through it. Neither can it be obliterated or rendered invalid by that which occurs subsequently. It stands outside time whilst requiring the specific historical elements of time and space for its articulation. It may refer to the past, but it is not held captive by it.

When we speak about truth and its relation to a painting or piece of sculpture we are speaking about the artist's ability to convey an essential dimension of reality present, and yet not present until articulated in the work. As a meaningful description and therefore a true statement, it is objectively present to be seen and touched, yet for all its individuality and originality as the act of creative intuition, it remains a statement which can be understood. If a work is limited to the totally subjective, either it will not be understood, or the total subjectivity will classify it as one of many examples of a like genre, which may tell us something about the state of the visual arts eg at the beginning of the 21st century, but tells us nothing about reality itself. A critic writing on Tracy Emin's latest exhibition and comparing the artist's 'mature' work with her earlier work stated that 'what we have now is the "content of an artistic vision"'. 'Content' here equals art focused on the artist. Here vision does not refer out but back to the self. It corresponds to a description Jean-Paul Sartre made of hell: a place where there is 'no exit' from the self. Truth implies the opposite: a freedom moving out and the communication of something fresh – an insight which enriches one's understanding of reality. Real vision, like truth, does not result in a kind of temporal cul-de-sac. It points to the future, not to the passing moment.

Intentionally lying close to the 'cutting edge' may be a recipe for achieving renown, but it is most certainly an indication of artistic vacuity. If in order to be understood and valued art has to be explained, located historically or structurally, identified *vis-à-vis* a particular artist; has it failed in its essential role as art – namely creating a vision – a way of seeing which extends beyond the present moment, or at least does not see the present as the latest version of the past? What Abraham Heschel describes as the attitude necessary to understanding the prophet could well be ascribed to the artist as a visual prophet, namely the necessity of seeing with insight:

> Insight is a breakthrough, requiring much intellectual dismantling and dislocation... a feeling for the unfamiliar... after much perplexity and embarrassment we come upon insight – upon a way of seeing the phenomenon from within. It entails genuine perception, seeing anew. He who thinks we can see the same object twice has never seen. Paradoxically insight is knowledge at first sight.[3]

---

[3] Abraham Heschel, *The Prophets*, p.xii.

Art and Humankind

Body and Soul:
Some Reflections on Art and Religion

TO MAKE ART IS 'to give form to the truth of reality in a language accessible to sight, touch and hearing'. This accessibility is unlimited; no one is excluded from its exercise; no one is excluded from an understanding of it. It is the most fully human of activities, a manifestation of the whole man, body and soul. The foundation of this essay rests on this principle, but its objective goes beyond this to a wider 'metaphysic' to show some of the relations which exist between art and spirituality. It is presented as a belief which is true, and hence as not one belief among many beliefs which are equally valid. The faith which provokes me to write this, the way of knowing which is essential to faith, is akin to that fundamental relationship which exists between art and spirituality, or to use the more old-fashioned term, which is probably more accurate, 'religion'. Both art and religion know things and express them in ways that elude the descriptive empirical sciences, and yet the objectivity they express actually comes closer to the foundations of truth based on nature and man's intrinsic way of knowing it, as a body informed by a soul – as a soul at one with a body. Spirituality, no more than art, can deny the essential place of the body in the metaphysical understanding of reality. For man cannot understand or express himself except as embodied, nor can he understand God except by recourse to his body. If it is true that the 'indestructibility of the body is the end of the works of God', and, as TS Eliot avowed in *The Rock*, 'the Lord who created must wish us to create', then the works of man must continue the works of God, and works of the body, which is immortal, must bear in some sense the quality of the everlasting, something which does not die and partakes of the eternity which is given to man in the Incarnation. An eminent theologian of the 20th century has noted that Christianity alone, eschewing a path to salvation relying solely on spiritual means, 'has found in mortal flesh the unsurpassable end of the ways of God'. One is saved body and soul. It is in weak and vulnerable flesh that man is saved. It is in matter and through matter that man creates art, an expression of truth to which the body contributes as much as the soul. What is essentially vulnerable and subject to change is lifted from its vulnerability in the artist's engagement with it, not by bypassing the creative material act by some purely cerebral conception (as proposed by Conceptual Art) but by the artist's subjection to the needs of the material; not by domination, but by, as it were, a 'mutual complicity' which is the artistic expression.

What unites art and religion most closely is perhaps a shared attitude: a certainty which cannot be verified; respect for, and a delight in, that which stands apart from us. This is an attitude little in contemporary vogue, where art is the artist, and its meaning can only be deciphered by reference to its 'creator'. It is the reverse of the religious stance, where the creator is known through his creation. This respect, which is part of the religious and aesthetic attitude, is by nature something primitive, and hence not exclusive, something fundamental to man – the ability to wonder and to learn. What the artist makes, what the religious person understands, is never something static. It is ever moving forward, not by acquisitive progress, but in discovery and a delight in the truth which has been 'seen'. In respect to God, it is an understanding which brings peace.

Yet there is another side to this shared attitude of the artist who makes and of the person who believes: it is the struggle which precedes the made thing, or the act of faith which leads to having faith.

It is the engagement of the whole person, body and soul, to express, or, in spiritual terms, to realise or recognise with surety. Before the thing is known or believed, in artistic terms before it is expressed, there is an awareness of something, a need to speak, be it with words or visually, a possibility which seeks to be understood and finalised or completed in the made object, in a belief which carries one forward. The struggle which precedes completion or vision shows the essentially active nature of art and faith, something which seeks further expression, greater understanding. It is never a settled matter. It is not always conscious. Indeed, for the child and the 'primitive', there is not the struggle, perhaps because there is not the same need for purification; one has not grown old in the ways of seeing. That is why the body is so important, for, aesthetically speaking, growing old is a matter of mind rather than body. The body grows old physically, but its spiritual élan is ever present. The soul (not the mind) remains in the form of the body. Artistically speaking, the body retains its native innocence, and the soul is, in a sense, without age.

What is essential to the birth and continued existence of both art and religion is a constant renewal. As far as religion is concerned, renewal is effected by means of the incorruptible soul which informs the corruptible body. This soul is not subject to time. It lives within time and through time but, in the sovereignty of its judgements, it also stands above time. Its task is to renew time through its actions. The renewal of artistic activity also involves continuation and change. These elements, change and rest (continuation), are like activity and contemplation. They represent the body and soul. In reality they cannot be distinguished, but remain one. In making art, in looking at art, continuation and change merge in judgement – a judgement is made in time and is influenced by it, and yet it seems to stand outside of it. To make a judgement is to make a statement of truth, which represents the present, refers to the past and reveals the future. It is 'outward', manifested in time, and hence bodily. It is an inward truth which is shaped by the human spirit. Truth, as the word denotes in Greek, is an unveiling of something which exists, and yet lies hidden. The artist is committed (even unknowingly) to this revelation, to this seeing anew. The essential reference to truth as 'unveiling' is at the heart of all artistic and religious expression – as something received, and perceived as something given. It is an understanding at once practical (active) and speculative (contemplative) that which is gazed on with appreciation. Essentially it is bearing witness in the most personal and deep-seated way possible – and yet having consequences of infinite proportion: revealing the truth to those who are willing to see.

The Sense of Touch Versus Conceptual Art

The painter 'takes his body with him' says Valery. Indeed, we cannot imagine how a 'mind' could paint. It is by lending his body to the world that the artist changes the world into paintings. To understand these transubstantiations, we must go back to the working, actual body – not the body as a chunk of space or a bundle of functions but that body which is an intertwining of vision and movement.[4]

Maurice Merleau-Ponty

THE MEDIEVAL PHILOSOPHER ST THOMAS Aquinas (1225–1274) considered touch to be the foundation of all the other senses to the extent that each sense could be said to involve touch, ie each sense involves contact with or touches the world in a manner specific to it. Amongst all the animals, man is the most perceptive in his sense of touch and the most intelligent men the most touch perceptive.

Aquinas goes on to explain that, as the intellective soul requires a body for sensation (all knowledge is based on information we gather through the senses) and that the body man possesses must correspond to his soul, whose grasp is of things infinite, just so man is equipped with '*ratio et manus*' – reason and hands. Man's hands are referred to as 'the tool of tools' – '*organa organorum*'. Hands and the sense of touch remain essentially body and yet they express soul. They express 'being in the world' in the mode which is particular to

---

[4] Maurice Merleau-Ponty *The Primacy of Perception*, p. 162.

them – a material mode, a mode which, although material, is in no way confined by its corporeality, but, rather requiring it, is able to speak in a way which exceeds the powers of the intellect alone. Each of the arts possesses this ability to speak its own language. Visibly and tangibly through matter, man expresses the 'two limits of creation' – matter and spirit. If reason can describe the workings of the body, it is also true that the body can describe, through its works, meanings which elude the mind but express the spirit.

These remarks lead us back to an initial idea taken from Aquinas's *Summa:* that human nature is an essential unity of matter and spirit. It is through the body and by means of matter that drawings, paintings, and sculptures are made. But how is it that a spiritual truth can actually be expressed more efficiently, more profoundly, by that which is essentially matter and also more completely than it can by means of an empirical, analytical statement? Because man *is* body and soul, there is a lack of accuracy and reality in a so-called artistic manifestation which does not incorporate the bodily dimension. This is why Conceptual Art is somehow unreal, and empty of expression. In trying to transcend the physical or locating one's expression solely in a concept, Conceptual Art actually impedes the possibility of conveying meaning. There is no objective reality to which to refer. Hence it is that any single work of Conceptual Art can be imputed as having an infinite number of meanings. The 'input' is totally from without in the sense of the viewers' projections. There is no sustaining reality to return to. The refusal of an ontological framework on which to base experience prevents any objective appraisal or appreciation. Reality itself has the status of mere projection, the result of a theory of knowledge which makes no claims concerning truth or value. Theory of knowledge has in fact replaced ontology.

When the artist has learnt to disregard or consider as limited what the hand can describe and the eye perceive, a destructive reversal takes place: relativism becomes objectivity, while the objective existence of truth and value become relative. The artist now doubts the capability of hand and eye, doubts the very existence of meaning. A breach is effected between body and spirit, such that the body can no longer speak through the spirit, nor the spirit through the body. But such negative directions fail to recognise that the fundamental unity between body and soul which manifests itself in a work of art is a physical expression of something spiritual. It finds its complement spiritually in what is called the 'doctrine of the spiritual senses'. In the history of spirituality, the doctrine of the spiritual senses represents a means of describing the act of contemplation by reference to the five senses. What is most interesting is that the spiritual act par excellence, ie contemplation, is depicted as belonging to the physical, to the body and its five senses; and the highest expression of the spiritual senses is what might be considered (as it is by Aquinas) its most basic sense – that of touch. It is precisely by reason of the immediacy of its knowledge that touch is evocative of the total 'possession' of the mystical state. To touch is to make immediate contact without intervention or distance. The sense of sight, with its attendant theories of 'illumination' as representative of contemplation may perhaps come more readily to mind. But sight still implies a distance between the object and the one who perceives. Touch transcends this distance in contact, in possession of its object. It does not examine at length, from afar, but knows immediately by experience. For Bonaventure (1221–1274), the medieval doctor of the spiritual senses, touch surpasses sight because of its unitive function. Thus, the most fundamental and basic of the senses is likewise that which is the most perfect and the most spiritual. Plotinus (AD205–270) also describes the act of contemplation as an act of touching when all distance is eliminated even to the distance between the object of perception and he who perceives. It is not by chance, notes Karl Rahner,

> that the sense of touch is used in preference to that of sight representing communion with God, a sense of a possession which produces satisfaction in a joy at once intimate and profound.

The 'possession' which comes about in the contemplative act can be described by the Thomistic notion of 'connaturality'. This is an ability demonstrated in the making of an object. In the same way that contemplation transcends the intellectual order, the artist transcends the expectations of an 'accepted' perception of the world. As Jacques Maritain says, 'In art as in contemplation, intellectuality at its peak goes beyond concepts and discursive reason, and is achieved through a congeniality or connaturality with the object, which love alone can bring about'. This connaturality is the result of the gift of wisdom, experienced in Thomas Heath's words as, 'an intuitive rush not given to the more laborious workings of reason'.

This 'connaturality' expresses itself then in a contemplative and practical way, that is to say, in judgement. 'Wisdom implies a certain rightness in judging according to divine norms. Now rightness in judging comes about in two ways, through the perfect use of reason, or through a certain natural kinship with the things one is judging about',[5] Thomas Heath writes in an appendix to his translation of the *Summa Theologica*. This is the judgement the artist engages in – a 'right judgement', intuitively 'his'. It is not a learned response or a technique employed. It is a singular observation, the expression of a relationship, perceptive and appreciative, between the artist and his work. It is a special understanding of it which he pursues. At its most 'elevated': it is the most direct. It is a natural and yet original congruence between what is perceived and what is depicted. The 'connatural' is not a rule to be applied in a given situation. There is no situation with a fixed response: 'every time there is the singularity of a new case which is in actual fact, unprecedented'.[6]

The basically non-analytic character of the aesthetic object provided Aquinas with an analogue fit to portray the highest gift of the Spirit, that of wisdom whose 'perfection is not understood

---

[5] *Thomas Heath, Summa Theologiae Vol. 35, Appendix 4.*
[6] *Jacques Maritain, Creative Intuition in Art and Poetry.*

by analogies with rational abstract knowledge but rather by... the experience of (being) grasped... by the beautiful'.[7] Elsewhere, Thomas speaks of divine knowledge 'as standing in relation to created things as the artist to his products'. Under both of these questions in the *Summa* there is reference to the production or existence of something that is the result of an act that is more than pure understanding or intellectual knowledge by reference to an act, either the act of divine creation which includes will or the act of judgement which is the result of the gift of wisdom. Both are likened to an artistic act, an act which is a direct seizing of reality, a proclamation of the truth. In the examples the physical is used to depict the most spiritual of realities. So also in an act of contemplation the analogy used is the artist at work. The soul's greatest act, that of charity, is the result of wisdom. Thomas's

> ...general conception of a gift (is) as an infused habit which makes man responsive to the movements of the holy Spirit and completes the work of virtue, not as regards the kinds of things accomplished but the *manner* of accomplishment. The gifts ensure a more direct, connatural, and intuitive manner of operation. Charity's gift is wisdom. [In wisdom] knowledge of the goodness of an object causes us to love it. Love then brings about a better kind of knowledge: this new appreciation deepens the love which in turn intensifies the appreciation and so on.[8]

And though this knowledge is 'inarticulate' it is also more 'accurate'. Art, as it were, mirrors the immediate grasp of the contemplative stance. Wisdom is described as a 'better form of knowledge', better because not purely intellectual but complete, expressed in act. Wisdom acts. Judgment engages the whole man, physical and intellectual. The gift of wisdom is not only speculative but practical

---

[7] *Thomas Heath, Summa Theologiae Vol. 35, Appendix 4.*

[8] Thomas Heath, *Summa Theologiae* Vol. 35.

(it makes). For the 'higher the virtue the further its extent' (*'aliqua virtus est altior tanto, ad plura se extendit'*), ie from the 'highest' to the most 'basic' of the physical sensations, that of touch. The material is not limited by its physicality any more than the body weighs down the soul, rather it (the body) is a source of enrichment to the soul. 'To be united to body is not to the detriment of the soul, but for its enrichment.'[9] The body regarded as such is not an encumbrance but the source of inspiration, 'physically' through what is learnt by the senses and 'spiritually' or creatively it is the instrument of the spirit. Man, a composite of 'reason and hands' (*ratio et manus*) 'can make a limitless range of tools with a limitless range of activities.' The work of art mirrors this 'limitless range'. This infinity of expression results when the whole man is engaged. And even in its highest expression, it is that which is most immediate and parallels, includes, the physical dimension which becomes its most eloquent spokesman. In order to tell the truth, the intellect must refer to the body.

Wisdom amongst the gifts of the spirit is considered the highest. And as we have noted for Aquinas, the higher the virtue the greater its extent: 'Wisdom spans from end to end and orders all things sweetly.'[10] In terms of aesthetics and specifically the visual arts, the spirit engages the body and the body expresses the spirit. The higher the spirit soars, the more profound is its scope to the extent that the most basic of faculties has the richest possibility of expression. It is not by reference to the intellect that the soul describes its being in the world it inhabits, but by the most basic of senses, that of touch, silently, perfectly. The more sublime the statement, the more profound the foundation. The more primitive the resonances, the more spiritual the effect. The soul's ambitus is by the hand and eye transcribing in visible, tangible marks its being in the world. The need for the hand does not limit expression but expands to infinity. By comparison the 'artistic expressions' of the conceptual approach

---

[9] Thomas Heath, *Summa Theologiae.*

[10] Wisdom 8:1.

appear impoverished, subjective and sceptical; rejecting judgment in preference for a transitory façade to which all manner of meaning can be imputed. The elusiveness of the 'idea' does not give it unlimited potential; for in the end there is no substitute for reality. The act of judgement is an affirmation of existence, and in terms of making art, it is the intuitive spirit which judges via hand and eye. In what sense could a judgment about art be applied to an idea? Artistic judgment is, by definition, formed in and by the senses. An idea is a conceptual, intellectual construct, detached from sense reference. 'Ideas' are quick, fast, instant gratification. If the senses are employed it is by process of bombardment. The hand, by comparison, is slow to move. Even at its quickest it has to pass via the material world. But that 'passage' has a spiritual dimension to which one can return. It leaves an enduring presence which can be both true and beautiful.

The *raison d'être* of Conceptual Art claims to be its unlimited scope for artistic expression. But is not this limitlessness rather an emptiness and therefore devoid of expression? Aquinas' ontology provides a different kind of infinity grounded in the concrete use of hand and eye, in touch, whose expression is as original and new as the individual who makes it, and as unlimited as the instances of time and space which give rise to it.

Why Artists Need Hands, and
the Process of Individuation

IN A WORLD WHERE images proliferate and can be made by any manner of means, one might ask why should any artist make things with his hands if it can be done more efficiently by some other means? Why need we go back to the true original source of things – the hand? What does the hand confer that the machine does not? The answer is individuality, singularity. The problem of art, the problem of its making, is concerned with the question of singularity, a question which involves originality, but which is more basic. It goes back to man's essential needs, both material and spiritual, a need for the concrete, for the singular, for what exists, instances whose individuality is materially fixed in time and space. The enjoyment which forms a part of the 'aesthetic experience' cannot be separated from the individuality of those objects which are the occasion of it. One does not take pleasure in an abstraction. The attraction or repugnance that one feels in looking at art is not a reaction to a general idea. It exists as a reaction to something very specific, an instance, a presence. What the viewer sees corresponds in some sense to what the artist creates. The viewer's needs are met by an expression in bodily form. The hands of the artist particularise and make concrete this form. The resulting object is not a copy of a pre-existing idea in the mind of the artist, the work does not exist before it exists. The object which exists is always more than any idea which preceded it, hence art is never a copy of an idea. Its physical nature precludes that. Concepts do not satisfy; an idea remains an idea, something universal. In the sense the eye can 'copy' an idea, but cannot express what the hand reveals. The real originality of any work will only be revealed through the hand.

The sense of touch, as St Thomas Aquinas noted, remains something basic and this allows it a great scope of expression. True originality lies here in physical terms, not in the bright ideas and 'shock tactics' of Conceptual Art which are a betrayal of the materiality of the object. Damien Hirst's *Spastic Girl*, for all its grandeur, remains an idea. What is mistakenly taken as originality in Conceptual Art is really a kind of mock presentation. What is being presented is not a work made by human hands, which has an integrity and existence of its own, but rather an idea which remains attached to, and in a sense, cannot be separated from the mind of the artist who produced it. Hence the accompanying relativity assumed in aesthetic judgments.

By contrast, objectivity frees; there is no 'vested' interest, only the truth of the object. It is in the handling of materials: paper, pencil, clay, whatever, that true originality consists. The conceptual approach illustrates an idea, but the ideas presented are like 'images adrift'; they have no existence of their own. It is not just a case of adding a third dimension to what is two-dimensional, but of realising that the two-dimensional has its source – '*origo*' (originality) – in the hand. It is something made, physical.

In the *Summa* of St Thomas Aquinas, the hands are referred to as the '*organa organorum*', 'the tool of tools'. We do not usually think of the hand as organ in the way that the eye is the organ of sight, 'a part of the body serving some vital function'. And yet the hand is described by Thomas as an organ. The accuracy of his description can be seen if we consider both the scope and the refinement of the powers of touch. This 'refinement' is due to the basic and primitive nature of the sense of touch, and includes its diversity, a kind of synchronicity, an ability to interpret and synthesise a vast array of things; hard, smooth, cold, still, dry, etc. Although Thomas uses the term 'organ' to refer both to touch and to the hand, it is to the latter that we usually attribute the sense of touch properly speaking. The hand is what actively touches; it both receives touch and makes it. It is in the hand that the sense of touch can be said to reside specifically. It is the hand that gives the 'lead' to the eye. It, the hand, verifies and locates. It is the point of immediate contact between the artist and the world, the source of the physical, and hence of the individually made object. But the hand is not the dumb instrument of the brain any more than the soul is the motor of the body. The two are not joined as two separate entities, but in an 'informed union', in scholastic terms a substantial union, real, whole, complete. This union is in some sense analogous to the artist's relation with his work, where the hand informs matter, instils life, not as a framed idea, but in union with the material. The hand does not impose on matter, but cooperates with it. For the material is an essential element in this union, even as the body is to the soul. This union is both material and spiritual, existing as one, expressing man's nature: soul and body. What man creates retains a likeness to him, in its individuality, in its singularity, for the hand cannot produce 'en masse'. It (the hand) is a defining instrument of volume and of line, of space and of mass, of quality of every kind. It sets limits physically with matter, but as a definer, as an originator, as that which individuates (to form into an individual entity), making whole and complete. It is the hand's 'innocence' which makes it the great originator.

Because of its primitive nature it is spared the 'saturation' which can befall the eye. It has remained primitive, 'innocent' as it were, because it is so basic, so all pervasive. Because of these traits it is the least susceptible to the influence of the mind, to the analytical or conceptual. And it is this 'natural innocence' which is indispensable to the wisdom of artistic expression. In what it does, the hand remains without equal, for it alone is both active and passive, completely physical, and yet imbued with an expressive means which is as transcendent as it is real, whose transcendence is transcendent in so far as it is real.

Much of the latter part of the 20th century, and the beginning of the 21st has seen a movement away from the figurative, and an ever-greater dependence on technology, a movement away from the made object, and a corresponding movement away from objectivity and a belief in what exists. At its beginning, the history of art records the depiction of a human hand, virtual sign of the unity of soul and body. The 20th century and the 21st have seen a denial of this unity, where the idea replaces the object, and art no longer has an inherent transcendence, rooted in time and place, but whose existence is denoted by the mere passage of time. The hand has become yet another 'tool among tools' – less efficient and primitive in its abilities. Yet it is precisely this 'primitiveness' centred in man's being, which allows the hand direct access to the imagination and to the infinite expressions of the human spirit.

PART THREE

Criticism

Spontaneity and Objectivity

A FEW YEARS AGO, a papal encyclical was published entitled *Veritatis Splendor*, which could be translated 'the beauty of truth' or literally 'the splendour of truth'. I would like to suggest in this short essay that spontaneity and objectivity are, as it were, the two scales of truth, the two sides of the balance of specifically artistic truth: one, spontaneity, conveying its infinite richness, its splendour, the other, objectivity, revealing its stability, its fidelity, its sureness. This *'splendor veritatis'* or *'veritatis splendor'* as it is in the original encyclical, is the soul of art.

The notion of splendour, what I have translated as the beautiful, need not and, in fact, must not be restricted to the 'beautiful', when beauty is synonymous with graciousness or loveliness, for the beauty of art is often not beautiful in this sense. The beauty of art is often an unexpected assault on what is visually accepted as the gracious or beautiful. Then it is beauty in all its objective and realistic 'candour' – the beauty of truth. But this realism of art is a tempered realism, perhaps not consciously so, often not consciously so. It is a realism which captivates the senses as much as the mind. Its power to captivate lies in its ability to render something as both familiar and yet totally new, so that, for example, the drawn chair is exactly right, and yet it is like no chair we have ever seen before. It is the product of a natural rather than a forced spontaneity (which strives for originality – what we could call a 'cutting edge originality'). The aesthetic realism which I am speaking of draws upon the two essential characteristics of art: spontaneity and objectivity. One could say as a natural phenomenon they appear in this order: spontaneity then objectivity, first that which manifests itself freely, uniquely (spontaneity) and yet is part of the universally recognisable enterprise which is art (objectivity). This art cannot be a copy, either of the world or of the artist's preconceived idea of the object which will eventually appear. Art appears as an act of correspondence between the artist and his materials. We might ask: how can a physical object be the bearer of truth? In what sense can a physical object express a logical notion: truth? At this point I would like to cite a fairly lengthy quotation from one of the most notable theologians of the last century, Hans Urs von Balthasar, and the first volume of his *Theo-Logic*: 'Truth of the World':

> Truth is not just a property of knowledge but a transcendent property of being, a fundamental quality and constituent structure of every being...which shares most intimately in all the depth and breadth of being and in all the degrees and forms of existent entities...

Hence the truth of art, the truth of the statement it makes, and its correspondence with reality, truly make it objective, able to make a true statement. To continue with von Balthasar:

> The reduction of the knowledge of truth to purely theoretical evidence drained of all vital personal and ethical decisions (and one can include aesthetic decisions at this point) so palpably narrows the scope of truth that it *ipso facto* loses its universality and, therefore, its very essence... Modern rationalism attempting to narrow the range of truth to a supposedly isolate-able core of pure theory, has exiled the good and the beautiful from the realm of the rationally verifiable, relegating them to arbitrary subjectivity

> or to a world of private belief and personal taste...
> Discourse remains at the level of the generally acces-
> sible, hence ultimately trivial, while the deepest
> questions of truth, which need decision and taste to
> be seen are buried under a silence of a false modesty...

The objectivity we speak of, therefore, when we talk about art is real and not metaphorical. It is not objectivity in the most narrow, limited, and restricted sense, that of a scientifically verifiable truth, but an objectivity which is a practical and living reality. Objectivity or truth, as its essential meaning would have it, is infinitely rich and variable. This is how the world is: infinitely rich, rich not as the figment of someone's imagination, but as a plenitude of a reality whose depths are never totally revealed. Truth must include all things and as such be concerned with each thing in its own specificity, and not as it is represented by a general law which is external to it. If then we treat objectivity – the objective world, reality – as truth itself, we must see this objectivity as it is naturally expressed, as it is seen, as it appears, and this needs be truth in all its spontaneity, as the unexpected. As the name indicates, spontaneity (from the Latin *'sponte'*, of one's own accord) is something that happens freely, naturally according to its nature, and individually. The subject is the source of spontaneity as the subject acts, as it is, and if the subject is an artist, as it makes, but the subject is also an object or objective in its manifestations and expressions; it can be understood, and appreciated by others. What is made, the work of art, is also a subject, a subject which exists in its own right, which must exist in its own right, apart from the artist, and be understood on its own terms, as it is.

Art – its making by the artist, its perception by the viewer, and its existence as an object in its own right – presents the case par excellence of the unity of subject and object, a unity of sympathy which is an expression of truth, of an implicit understanding at once physical and spiritual: the spontaneous-ness of the artist witnessing to an availability to the matter in which he works (this is why an object cannot be limited to a merely conceptual expression. Man's truth is both physical and spiritual, as is the object he makes, the object he sees). The object, the work, is open and receptive to the meaning given by the artist. The object is the child of the artist, but it is not a creation *ex nihilo*, 'out of nothing'. It is a work which has joined in its own creation. Its expression, its meaning, is not one imposed from without, but the result of an openness which must exist on the part of the artist and object. Spontaneity on the part of the artist implies a readiness to receive the world, to form it in conjunction with itself. Essentially the relationship is one of a dialogue with the world which precludes the notion of art as merely idea. Much contemporary art is pure monologue, excluding object, excluding viewer. Dialogue assumes an equal footing, an openness, a freedom. Spontaneity itself is an expression of freedom, a freedom which allows objectivity. The artist and his work are part of this objective world. The essentially mysterious nature of truth, that there is always more to be revealed, is part of this objectivity. For reality is plenitude. As indicated in the Greek word for truth – *aletheia* – truth is an unveiling of what is, what objectively exists. The artist assists this unveiling, not by a carefully practised technical approach, but by an openness to what is there, what he sees, to the materials he uses, and by an openness to himself, by a free response. Spontaneity is this free response. It is not a free or sudden response, *ex abrupto*, but one which has been influenced in a multitude of ways which constitute the history of each individual. The history of art itself is an expression of a synthesis of these two elements: the 'spontaneous', that irreplaceable and singular element which is the contribution of the artist, and objectivity, that network of factors observable from 'cave art' to the present day, which is the expression of man's being in the world and that visual language which can be readily understood even as it eludes any definition. Both these elements, spontaneity and objectivity, persist in a statement of artistic truth, which is ever new yet whose value consists in a supra temporal and transcendental dimension – one which manifests itself necessarily as a specific and individual existing reality. The value of art as a bearer of truth lies in its ability to impart these two aspects of meaning, namely the universal and the particular, in a way which expresses the perfect unity of soul and body in a language whose accuracy could be said to be without parallel. For the language of artistic truth is the expression of the whole person, whose expression is at once spontaneous and objective.

Relativism: Art Without Object

TE HULME, IN A lecture given on modern art in 1914, said: '*The art of a people will run parallel to its philosophy and general outlook.*' And so it is. If one has to think of an attitude which best characterises our present age it is relativism – a world without anchor. Coupled with this general outlook is an attitude of skepticism – the ironically avowed inability to be sure of anything, to know what is true, let alone to be able to make judgements concerning value, least of all aesthetic value. I say 'ironic' because the skepticism which is believed and practised (basically religious terms) has a certain doggedness and grit about it. Just as there are only 'devout Catholics', there are only 'convinced skeptics'. Much of what goes as art today is artistic activity, something to be participated in. The contemplative, wondering dimension has disappeared because the object itself has disappeared and been replaced by an art of active engagement – a moving, dynamic art. The bright idea syndrome of Conceptual Art has become boring and is giving place to a performing visual art. Henri Bergson in his theory of art said: 'The more we are preoccupied with living the less we are inclined to contemplate, and the necessities of action tend to limit the field of vision.'

But what has all this to do with relativism? What does relativism have to do with action? If anything, one might feel justified in thinking that relativism's allowing everyone to have a different idea would actually broaden the field of vision, or our evaluation of it, rather than narrow it. Is this 'vision', 'perception', spoken of, concerned with the objective, the subjective, or both? Does belief in an objective standard actually narrow our vision as relativism would have us believe? Clearly relativism focuses on the subject, the one who perceives, who can believe whatever he feels like believing. But does the possibility of believing anything and everything actually give breadth of vision? Where perception has lost its objective foundation does it still remain perception? Does the object have a place in all of this? Is there still a place for the object in the artistic vision of the present day? And if there is not, is this symptomatic of the general outlook of the times in which we live? The eminent contemporary theologian, Joseph Ratzinger, describes the present situation as a 'crisis' – (etymologically a time of judgement) existing

> due to the fact that the connecting link between the subjective and the objective realm has disappeared, that reason and feeling are drifting apart, and that both are ailing because of it. The result is an unhealthy over development in the realm of the technical and pragmatic knowledge in that of basic fundamentals, and thus the balance between them is disturbed in a way that may be fatal to humanity...[11]

Hard words, but are they true? Objectivity is concerned with truth, something that obtains and exists apart from the individual 'me'. Can there be any sense to the term 'value' if it lacks this quality of objectivity? Is objectivity really necessary to art and if it isn't is this yet another way of saying, is there anything particularly valuable in art, a reason why we need it? If objectivity is missing, either because we believe such a thing as objectivity doesn't exist or because there is no longer anything we can point to out there, what are the consequences for mankind? Does the predominant relativist climate indicate that art is in a state of crisis? And what are the artistic manifestations of this crisis?

---

[11] Joseph Ratzinger, *Truth and Tolerance, Christian Belief and World Religions.*

An example: last autumn there was an exhibition of the work of Matthew Barney at the Serpentine Gallery. In a headline from the arts column of the *Daily Telegraph* of the 18th September 2007, Barney is spoken of as 'a visionary straining at the leash'. He is further described as 'perhaps the most original artist alive'. Does 'the most original artist alive' imply different from the rest? Or are there more of this 'original' type to follow? Is the fact that there is a lead article on him and that he has an exhibition at one of the main London galleries indicative? His exhibition was described as 'one of the most important cultural events of the autumn'. The word 'cultural' is significant – what is taking place is part of a 'cultural ethos' and is therefore important because of that.

Traditionally, the artistic work has always existed in its own right and apart. Even Duchamp's *Urinal* is a statement – it is 'there'; it isn't 'taking place'; it isn't an activity. By contrast *Matthew Barney: Drawing Restraint* (the complete name of the project) is a feat, an artistic feat compared in the article with Michelangelo's painting the Sistine Chapel – artistic because it is painted by an artist, feat because it is difficult to do.

The work of Matthew Barney and numbers of others like him is indicative of the fundamental shift that has taken place in art. It is the artistic process rather than the object of art, which is being presented for our admiration. Art has become performance; its ontological status has vanished and value given to the 'enactment of the artistic process'. Art has become entertainment, something that is done between other activities for amusement. Now amusement is a subjective affair, what amuses me may not amuse you, and what may amuse me at one moment may not amuse me at another. It is a relative matter. The viewer chooses his amusement and, as he need not refer to anything or anyone in this matter except himself, there is nothing binding on him, no judgment is implied. The artistic object in the traditional sense, has always been something stationary or at least material. The necessary physical stability inherent in a work of art demands or has demanded a corresponding stillness and attention in the viewer. It does not 'happen'; it is. This has changed. And because the 'critical stance' of the relativists (in one sense an impossibility) demands 'flexibility', the art of artistic process and hence Barney's work performance corresponds neatly with the relativist's attitude. If the onus of referring to an existing object in making critical judgments is done away with, the result is that the very existence of criticism itself is called into question. It is ironic that in a world where only that which can be verified is accepted, artistic criticism should be so adamant in eschewing any form of objectivity.

This is why the situation has become so critical. One's connection with an enduring reality has been denied and in a sense even communication itself has been called into question: we cannot know, we cannot speak or will not. The individual is left with himself; entertainment has become a substitute for reality and truth. That art now manifests itself as artistic activity rather than art per se affirms TE Hulme's belief stated at the beginning of this essay 'that the art of a people will run parallel to its philosophy'. Relativism implies change; it is *ipso facto* conditional and assumes no continuity, but objectivity depends on continuity; there must be a constant, the anchor of truth so to speak. To judge is precisely to seek the truth – and seeking the truth means abiding in it and being able to communicate it. Objectivity is part of the essence of judgment, of aesthetic judgments as much as of any other judgment.

The disappearance of the work of art as existing object has made judgment impossible so to what do we refer? If relativism is merely saying: what is good to me is good to me, in what sense has a decision or judgment been made? If art is no more than process and activity, there is no need to make judgments, no need to do anything except describe my feelings at any given moment.

Because contemporary man seems to be riddled with doubt, he will not commit himself by a judgment, because judgment denotes responsibility. It denotes stability. An art which will not 'objectivise' itself in an action, which endures beyond the activity itself, *ipso facto* also refuses to commit itself to a judgment – relativism is the only appropriate stance to take. Correspondingly art of performance replaces the art of lasting value, entertainment replaces contemplation, reflection, and perceptive responsibility. Again, Matthew Barney provides an example:

> For him what is valuable is not so much the finished product, as the tension between the desire to create and the discipline required to funnel that desire into making art. This is why petroleum jelly (*sic*) is such an important symbolic material for Barney.

Would petroleum jelly then be an appropriate *ikon* for relativism? There is an intensity about all this, but no seriousness, a whimsicalness but not delight. The art of any period is the product of the generation that produces it. What appears to be missing at the present moment is the connective link between the subjective and the objective. There is an intensity about all this but no seriousness, a whimsicalness but no delight. If 'the art of a people does correspond to its philosophy and general outlook' is there any future for art beyond the present moment? Yes, if the connective link between the subjective and the objective realms are reinstated: yes, if the equilibrium between reason and feeling is restored. There are signs, at least in some quarters that this is happening.

Boredom and 'The Art of Change'

IT SEEMS THAT the word 'boredom' has no etymological record prior to the 18th century, although the notions of 'ennui', and even more of 'acedia', have a very ancient heritage. Two great monastic writers of the 4th century AD, Cassian and Evagrius, devote a considerable amount of space to the subject of 'acedia' – it being a spiritual illness to which monastic persons are especially prone. The difference between 'boredom' and its more ancient forebears 'acedia' and 'ennui' seems to lie in the fact that the former – boredom – implies no judgement regarding the person suffering from it, whilst the older depictions of the 'illness' definitely do imply a moral responsibility on the part of the subject. This fact itself probably involves a further implication, namely that contemporary man suffering from boredom seems to eschew any responsibility as a moral agent either for his state of mind or the surroundings in which he finds himself. Michael Hanby, in an article in the review journal *Communio*, defines boredom in the following way: 'the failure of the world to be compelling to a subject ostensibly entitled to such an expectation, and a failure and incapacity on the part of the subject to be compelled' (entitled – if one is bored, it is a reaction to a boring state of affairs which is not one's fault – '*divertimento*' should be readily available).[12] Boredom might be described as life without change, where 'sameness' is the norm. So far it has been assumed that life is actually as the subject finds it: namely 'boring'. It implies nothing about the subject or

---

[12] 'The Culture of Death, the Ontology of Boredom, and the Resistance of Joy', *Communio* Vol. 31.2 Summer 2014.

why he sees everything as being the same, nor whether the world is actually as he sees it: boring, tedious, etc.

Now, a life without change, a life of boredom, is not the same thing as a stable life or a life of calm. Stability is necessary if such things as diversity, difference, contrast, interest can be noticed at all, or, in reference to art, can be appreciated and employed. There must some stable foundation, specifically a foundation of sound judgement (which is not the same thing as a rational account of sound judgement). Another way of describing aesthetic judgement is the ability to appreciate the good and the beautiful. It is an ability which is connatural and does not refer to a specialised competence. The naturalness of the ability bespeaks its stability. It also indicates that aesthetic judgement comes from, and refers to, an objective reality. Both aesthetic appreciation and judgement are a faculty of the human person, be he artist or viewer. But both can be undermined so that the good is no longer seen as good, objective and true, but a mere figment of the imagination, and not an imagination which actively, if unconsciously, cooperates with judgement and appreciation to produce and value something of aesthetic worth, but an imagination which sees change and difference, be it good or bad, as valuable in itself. This is the imagination which succumbs to the malaise of boredom. To those who suffer from boredom the cause appears to be exterior and there is the further implication that it is the world that is at fault and responsible for the boredom. If the world were different the boredom would disappear. A change is all that is required and all will be well. Or so it would seem. Yet boredom soon catches up and induces the bored individual to make yet another change in the fruitless search to eliminate boredom. The art world, and artists in particular, have come to be caught up in this syndrome of external change as a solution to an internal problem, namely: an impairment of our aesthetic mode of judgement (one mode of a generally impaired judgement) and, more fundamentally, a disbelief in the ability to judge and believe in the existence of an objective referent for this judgement. What we have is a destabilisation of the most fundamental of human faculties, our ability to know, judge, and appreciate.

What of the problem of boredom from the artist's point of view? Boredom would hardly be thought to be the ideal milieu for artistic creativity – the artist is no longer interested in what he is doing. He is engaging in change for change's sake, to do something new and different, not because the work itself actually requires a change, but, because the art world prefers shock and surprise, it therefore requires that the artist do something different. The very essence of art entails being able to judge, and so vary what he does or change completely – albeit on an intuitive level – the difference, distinction, comparison, contrast, etc in his/her work. These things the artist must employ and the audience must see. But all of these essential artistic dimensions are not equivalent to change, nor will change ensure them. Tedium, or boredom, describes an already existing general ambience in which the artist finds himself, for which he considers himself not responsible, and to which he ascribes his inability to be creative. But the root of this tedium is not so much in inappropriate surroundings, which, it is true, could be conducive to boredom, but an attitude to the surroundings and a belief that there is nothing at all 'out there' which is intrinsically good, beautiful and worthy of sustained interest. Because the artist is unable to find anything of intrinsic worth in the world about themselves to sustain them in their artistic endeavours, change is accepted as an alternative. But change simply issues in yet more boredom, because although change may bring difference, it does not necessarily bring quality. This is so because the recognition of quality entails both judgment and appreciation, neither of which exist independently from the perceiving subject who both judges and appreciates. Being at the very core of human perception in its widest sense, it is strange that the fundamental faculties of judgement and appreciation appear to be absent in the very people whom one would expect to be the most sensitive to their presence, namely artists and critics. Reliance on the use of change in one form or another will not fill this lacuna of judgement nor alleviate the boredom entailed by it. The existence of a change or difference can be nothing more than the presence of novelty. This is not the same thing as a change initiated as the result of a perception based on judgement. The judgment, which is fundamental to art, can be conscious in so far as one can allude to it or give aesthetic reasons for the choices made, but essentially it is a judgment which works above and below reasoned conscious decision. It is more the case of a discovery, an uncovering, a revelation which is perceived and shared. Mere change will not stimulate discovery any more than it will produce good art, and it can never be a substitute for it. There is something fundamental lacking where one's reliance is founded on change alone, namely an absence of belief in the objectivity and aesthetic worth of human perception. Such a lacuna is more likely to result in an attitude of domination and control, a frantic activity, and ultimately the very boredom it seeks to assuage.

But is art created in order that boredom might be alleviated? And if so, is the 'art of change' the most reliable remedy for this boredom? Damien Hirst has told us: 'there has only ever been one idea in art, and that is to communicate what it is like to be alive today.'[13] Hirst's own art assuredly verifies the latter of these two statements. Control, domination, ceaseless activity, instantaneous change, are all part of what it means to be alive today. They also figure largely in Hirst's *modus operandi*: *'I'm designing everything to a very high level, and nothing leaves this studio until it is exactly what I want.'* Hirst has a *'fear of things standing still'*. And he assures us that his paintings *'never stand still and they never bore you'*. For to merely look at something implies a boring exercise; it takes time, and the more time something takes the more boring it becomes. Yet in order to consciously register anything, one has to slow down. Speed has a

---

[13] Cassandra Jardine, *Daily Telegraph*, 10 September 2008.

numbing effect. With speed the ability to concentrate, let alone judge, evaporates; everything becomes a blur. Eventually what develops is a plane of boredom, what one might call the 'uniformity of change', the paradoxical situation where there is no change because there is only change, and no time to judge and reflect, to individuate. If these essential traits of judgement and reflection which means taking the time to look, to compare, to contrast, and finally to choose, are missing or atrophied through a lack of use, then no amount of change will eliminate the boredom which is the result of their absence.

Technology and Technique Versus Art

IF ONE GLANCES through Phaidon's two encyclopaedic volumes on contemporary art, *Vitamin P: New Perspectives in Painting* and *Vitamin D: New Perspectives in Drawing*, it is noticeable that two 'styles' or 'themes' seem to predominate: one having a political or sexual orientation, the other having a technological background. In a sense, both these types rely on or take their *raison-d'etre* from something outside of art. And both determine the art that is to follow. Both 'orientations' precede the work, rather than being coexistent with it. And both lack that 'cohesive trust' that should exist between form and content; rather there is a kind of domination either on the part of the subject matter, be it political or sexual, or on the part of the methodology. As though no longer able to speak for itself, the work of art is presented as requiring some sort of outside support: either a visual technique, a skill, or a verbal explanation in the form of a graphic message. The 'graphic message' is in a sense both the form and the content, yet it does not form a natural whole so much as push an issue, note an agenda, which only uses art as an instrument rather than allowing it to exist in its own right. In this case, the work of art is rendered 'plausible', 'acceptable' by the 'graphic message' which is attached to it. The image, being visually mute, allows the message to have precedence. The message, not the image, does the speaking. Any art which may be present in a work often is covered over by the use of technology or completely obliterated by it. For art to have credence in the contemporary world, if we are to go by Phaidon's two volumes, it must either be 'slick' or have some specific political or moral agenda. What has been unnecessary to art as from prehistoric times to the 20th century has become a necessary adjunct to it. Evidence of that essential quality of art, that sense of wonder or uniqueness which is part of its nature is no longer sufficient cause to gain it acceptability. Contrary to what we are told in the introduction to *New Perspectives in Drawing*, namely that: 'With drawing we never lose the sense of wonder', it is precisely this sense of wonder which seems to be lacking in the book.[14] Why does a child draw? Why does a caveman draw: to make something his own, to recount visually how this seems to him and in turn to share that impression, to give what could not be had in any other manner to someone else. It is not to explain or analyse that he draws, but to express, to appreciate, to make individual, to appropriate not by taking exclusive possession of something, but by creating and so giving: the pleasure of making, of seeing 'what is right'. None of these qualities are a feature of technique.

What technique and technology do is to make void the essential individuality of the artistic image, or object. This is because they limit the artist's contact with the work, that is to say a direct, physical and sense-inspired contact, wherein the work gradually takes on its individuality; adding its own natural elements, contributing as much through the difficulties it poses as through any positive benefits a particular material may have to offer. Technology prevents this intimate correspondence between artist and work which is necessary to artistic generation.

Why do we make art? What purpose does it serve? When the cave man drew a hand, he knew it was not a real hand. Is making art not more than the fulfilment of some psychological need? And if what is done can be explained in words, do these words ever replace or even approach saying what is meant in what the hand does? We live in a world dominated by technology and, through it,

---

[14] Phaidon Editors, *Vitamin D: New Perspectives in Drawing*, Introduction.

we are able to communicate in many useful things. But what do we communicate and can we communicate what the hand does, what the hand feels and what the eye sees; what we understand but cannot tell in any other way? Even if we were able to create everything by means of technology and obliterate any real need for the hand's impress, and could, by a spoken word alone bring into existence all that is needful, would it be sufficient? Would the spirit not require more, and also the body? The hand and its act of making are, as it were, an indissoluble bond between body and soul, and, if the body was no longer joined to the soul through art's concrete expression, would this not induce a slow death which had repercussions on mankind. Technology has moved things along in this direction. It can gratify a mind separated from body, it can even gratify to a certain extent a body separated from mind. But it cannot gratify or fulfil the human soul, the human spirit, the unity of mind and body. Art does this, while we live here below.

Religion and faith also require this unity of soul and body, at least in a Judeo-Christian context. Even though faith, and its expression religion, must go beyond the terrestrial domain of art, it requires art as a preparation for the journey to a more elevated state. This 'preparation' is essential; it is not an optional 'extra'. How we live determines how we shall live and this includes humbly accepting and rejoicing in our inability to know, analyse and explain everything. Art is an admission of this joy which is the foundation of that wonder which art requires. It is precisely this wonder which is absent from most of contemporary art. The fact that analysis, justification, and so much explanation is necessary to today's art indicates how far away from art's natural sources we are. The amount of technique and technology employed in the production of present day art testifies to this. The use of technique, however, is not new. From the Renaissance onwards, its presence can be seen to an ever greater extent. In the words of Hans Urs von Balthasar, 'the modern world has... reduced the natural rightness of things (and one could say one's ability to make and see them) into a mathematical quantum... It has equalised, quantified, depersonalised, and formalised human life. Technology is the result (and the cause as well) of this depersonalisation and formalisation... Modern aesthetics has contributed too to this depersonalisation, having reduced poetry and art to formalist exercises or private expressions marginal to the deeper concerns of existence...'[15] This depersonalisation of the artistic object goes hand in hand with a universal relativism which pervades all aspects of contemporary life. Relativism, one might say, is the ultimate depersonalisation, contributing as it has to a disbelief in the objective validity of the true, the good and the beautiful. Where there is no wonder, where things can be wholly explained there is no beauty. Where there is no truth or belief there is no art or reason to make it, because art requires the personal, the real and believable, as much as it does the beautiful, not as a representation of a believed – in reality, but as a new, true, and objective expression and appreciation of reality. This expression is not the effect of a subjective disposition, but an appearance that can be appreciated and valued. 'Beauty breaks forth from the form itself',[16] not from the subject's perception of it, as the relativists would maintain. 'The content does not lie behind the form (as an explanation of it) but within it.'[17] Technology itself represents this fact, but because the form it makes is every form and any form, it is no specific form and therefore lacks that essential trait of art: specificity, which one philosopher refers to as its 'logical elusiveness', ie that quality which renders it unsuitable to the needs of technology. For technology can reproduce a type or indicate a technique, but it cannot create.

The idea that art is by its nature something original and different, and therefore specific has been modified in contemporary aesthetics

---

[15] Hans Urs von Balthasar, *The Glory of the Lord* Vol 3.

[16] Ibid.

[17] Hans Urs von Balthasar. *The Glory of the Lord* Vol 1.

to mean that art must be 'original', no matter how banal, boring or insipid that 'originality'. In this case 'originality' becomes a type itself. Originality of this kind has come to be the *raison d'être* of art to the exclusion of any sense of form, charm, or 'comeliness'. If 'originality' cannot be found in the actual object, then an explanation or justification in the form of concept or artistic criticism can be used as a 'good second'; and what cannot be justified *'sui generis'* as form in art can be justified by words alone, where words replace images and concepts replace matter.

Another aspect of our technologically inspired contemporary society is its increasing use to the extent that it has gradually changed the whole way we look at time and how we use it. Technology has virtually come to be if not synonymous with speed, as least one of its outstanding characteristics. So that with the advent of technology and its fixation with speed and proficiency, and the very latest or 'newer' the thing the better; art that is not representative of the 'cutting edge' phenomenon is considered of no account. That art should be timeless ie demonstrative of beauty and that which is ever true, becomes incomprehensible where the very meaning of words 'beauty' and 'truth' are no longer reckoned as having any applicable meaning. Art has been simplified and mechanised, not in any spiritual sense but as something replaceable and reproducible, so again lacking specificity. There is no time for hand and eye that work at their own dictated speed, be it quickly or slowly and to a natural rhythm, where there is an over concern with speed. Technology represents time – *'tempo non-moderato'*. Primitive art is oblivious of time. The child too is oblivious of time and in a certain sense like God experiences all time as present. For technology there is no present; all is completed before it is begun, or never allowed to begin as always ahead. In a real sense one is separated from oneself and what one does in a technological ethos; one either lives in the past or in the future. To say art is timeless is to say that it is ever present.

Related to technology as a kind of sub-species is the phenomenon of 'technique' which is the use of skill, or an ability to do something, which can in turn be taught. There is a certain exclusivity about technique, for although a technique can be taught, not everyone can do it. This ability 'to do' or 'to make things look like they are' is considered acceptable and a way of proving that one has acquired the technique. However, one might say that the whole point of art is to show that things are actually different from what they are thought to be, or at least a good deal more than they are thought to be. What is considered acceptable is precisely the 'thinkable', the 'usual'. Here again the specific is lacking, the non-generic. This ability to wield a technique assumes an ability to analyse and to provide a method which can be used to represent something. This became a hall mark of the Renaissance and the rise of scientific interest. And the rise of an interest in the natural sciences came to mean also a corresponding decline in the 'metaphysical' way of looking at the world and that general attitude of 'respect' for those parts of life which science has so often tried to explain away as non-existent or of no account, or as a merely 'subjective' phenomenon. 'And with the death of metaphysics, the arts too have died off unnoticed, in that they are increasingly subordinated to the methodology of the natural sciences.'[18] With the learning of a technique one is said to acquire 'mastery' over something but to create is not to acquire mastery. It is not and cannot be an act of domination. It is rather co-operation between subject and object. Creation comes easily to the child, but not to the adult. The latter too readily assumes the air of a technician. Now it might be thought that the artist in his maturity will have gained a certain technical mastery over his material, something a child for lack of experience cannot do. But hopefully the artist in his maturity will have transcended this need for technical mastery and instead bear the true fruit of maturity: that

---

[18] Hans Urs von Balthhasar, *Explorations in Theology* Vol 3.

fullness of wonder which is natural to the child. As Michelangelo grew to artistic maturity his art became simple and even primitive in aspect. If one compares the *Buonarroti Pietà* to the *Rondanini Pietà*, his last work, this becomes obvious. The whole posture of a traditional *pietà* has been changed and the details simplified. The Virgin bears her son on her shoulder as He had born the cross. The movement towards artistic maturity shown here is not the acquisition of an ever more refined mastery over marble, but rather the contrary. The surface of the sculpture is rough, almost crude, yet the balance is perfect. The movement described here rather than being towards an exterior refinement is rather a movement inwards both spiritually and even physically (in that one is aware of an inner weight bearing – an inner balance). As the artist reached the maturity of his artistic expression his work became more interior, not in any narcissistic sense, but rather in a simplicity of expression, only possible through the shedding of that technical expertise which some like to associate with art. The true artist in his maturity will, like the child, create art naturally, unhampered by the need for expertise, but creating according to an inner dynamic which is truly open to the world, free from the regimentation of technology, technique, and the artificial need to be new and original, but open to the needs of the inner spirit.

The Importance of the Subjective: the True Meaning of Originality

THE QUEST FOR ORIGINALITY is not new, although it is pursued with great intent by much of contemporary art. To be 'original', to emphasise one's individuality and difference – in a sense this is a global pursuit, at least in the western world. What is usually a metaphysical 'given', namely that everyone and everything is different by the mere fact that he, she or it is embodied, has become virtually the *raison d'etre* of the current output of the world's art. Damien Hirst's *Diamond Encrusted Skull*, 'valued' at £50,000,000, has its predecessor in Duchamp's *Urinal*. Is the originality in the price or the artefact? A critic of the *Daily Telegraph* called Hirst's *Skull*: 'the most significant work of the decade' (a sign of the times that: art = money), and further adds, quite rightly, 'the entire meaning of the... skull is embodied in its price.' Here 'originality' equals the price the work can fetch. Duchamp, more honest in his intentions perhaps, equates originality with shock or outrage. The Futurists followed a similar path, as also the Dadaists.

'Originality' as such in its true artistic sense, is fundamentally different. Firstly and significantly, it cannot be sought – it is a given. Once it is sought it vanishes (see Picasso on originality). In today's avid search for originality, the artist substitutes his or her perception of the world's perception of himself/herself for the work. The work has no independent existence apart from the artist. It has a 'sell by date' determined by the prevailing fashion, which is inevitably replaced, and this at a greater and greater speed. But an essential aspect of art, and upon which its very independence is founded, is its spontaneity. Something which is spontaneous, although presenting itself as entirely new and without precedent, is basically a natural impulse, coming from within, without external stimulus. Spontaneity is something whose source lies within. Something within the artist responds to the world without. That response has no precedent. Spontaneity is by definition unpredictable. To determine its outcome in advance is to falsify it, to disconnect it from the artist and to sever that essential relationship between subject and object. The source of the spontaneous gesture is the artist, yet the artist is not a replacement for his art.

From an aesthetic point of view, which is more important, the artwork or the artist? We do not know who was responsible for the Caves of Lascaux, nor the frescoes in the catacombs. Does that matter as far as the art is concerned? Is the knowledge of the artist's identity of any importance in terms of our aesthetic appreciation of these two divergent examples of art? I think not. In our own day, the cult of celebrity, another form of 'economic splendour', has replaced the objective value of the work itself. Beauty as such no longer seems to be of any significance. It no longer has a role to play. The artist has replaced his art. There is no longer a 'virtue' in beauty (virtue in its etymological sense as *virtus* ie the strength or power). Beauty's natural course – *ambitus* – which is as infinite as the human spirit itself, has been chained to a cultural outlook where quality is defined in terms of fame and economy; fame determined by the price tag attached to what is produced, even if the artistic product is merely conceptual – an idea (the more outrageous the better). It is not that these factors, the use of shock and outrage have not existed in the past, but rather that they seem to have replaced the very *raison d'etre* of art itself. Originality in the contemporary sense of the word has replaced the art work itself. It is strange that although art no longer seems to require a human agent, that is to say the traditional source of a human hand and eye (for now it can be mass produced and even not produced ie merely 'thought up'), yet its originality is never questioned. The irony of it is that, the more remote, bizarre, or manufactured the product, the more conceptual and notional it is, the more the work merits the description 'original' – but 'origin' from where, from what? The work of art has become something without roots or source. It has been replaced by the artist and he himself has been replaced by a current idea, whose excellence or value (again an etymological comparison is of interest – value from *valere*, to be strong, as with virtue and *virtus*) is a monetary consideration rather than an aesthetic one.

However the notion of 'strength' is still a physically apposite characteristic in much contemporary art, although no longer in an aesthetic sense ie as having a capacity or ability to effect awe, wonder, and admiration in the viewer by its beauty, but rather by its sheer size. Big is beautiful! Many pieces are grandiose – the Tate's Turbine Hall, architecturally speaking, is necessary to cope with the sheer size of the pieces as with eg Miroslaw Balka's *Black Hole 'How it is'* or Doris Salcedo's *Crack in the Floor*. Allied to this physical attribute of the contemporary art scene, namely magnitude, is that of the technical impeccability and engineering skill associated with it. There is a 'faultlessness' about everything and with that a 'remoteness' which 'stands aloof' and disassociates itself with human frailty and so also artistic individuality. Art is an exercise in skill, an acquired skill. This problem is not new – and is yet another example of the artist replacing his art, but in this exchange the artist has suffered. He/she has forfeited his 'aesthetic soul' (and perhaps his spiritual soul, noting the repercussions of the aesthetic dimension) for a skill which soon passes out of fashion. Artistic integrity, as well as any other sort of integrity is not a matter of fashion or style.

Just as the term 'originality' has literally lost touch with its source so also the term subject or subjective has become 'merely subjective'. It is not that the notion of the subjective has been replaced by that of the objective, for the latter has disappeared altogether and no longer exists, but precisely that the objective element which underlies the subjective, has been replaced by a fleeting whim, and so the subjective, too, has been disparaged and belittled. What is subjective is no longer a matter of serious consideration. The more or less present usage of the word subjective dates from the early 18th century. Prior to that subject, subjectivity, had a literal sense, coming from the Latin word *subjacere*, to be under, to be fundamental, foundational, ie that upon which something rests. Subjective is then comparable in its etymological meaning to 'original' – from *origo* to arise out of, to have a source.

In art, there are two subjects ie two individuals: the artist and his work. In artistic activity, the artist or his work may predominate at any given time, set the pace, create obstacles, but ultimately the outcome depends on the interaction of the two. There is and must be an intrinsic relationship between artist and work. This relationship by nature intrinsic, has become, it would seem, almost entirely extrinsic, determined by outside factors obscuring a basic and essential relationship between art and artist. It may be that the artist as subject dominates, eg as with Tracy Emin's tabloid display of personal memorabilia, or it may be that an artistic work becomes a kind of genus eg Damien Hirst's shark in formaldehyde. In either case the intrinsic specificity of the work and subjectivity of the artist is betrayed, ie in the case of Tracy Emin, both she and her art have become equivalent to tabloid memorabilia. In the case of Damien Hirst, his sharks have become a type; there are not new and different sharks showing a development or a possible influence; there are just sharks. In both cases, the subject matter has taken the place of the individual work of art or alternatively the artist has replaced the work. The subject or content has become the individual work. The formal aesthetic aspect is no longer of import. Rather a theme or subject matter, a type, something general has been made to stand in for the individual thing. Form has been replaced by content. Formal considerations have to a greater extent disappeared giving way to content or thematic control from outside.

The contemporary uses of the terms original and subjective, although intending to indicate the individual person or thing, and also placing value upon 'individuality' as indicating an excellence, have instead bypassed the individual – be it person or thing – and replaced these with the current type, the fashion of the present moment or the latest artistic celebrity. Hence, a particular relationship between the artist and his art (itself a constantly changing phenomenon, internal, specific, and *sui generis*), has been severed and replaced by external criteria, determined from without – often on a global dimension. This global dimension of creativity appears as an ubiquitous celebration of the artistic ego; and the self-consciousness of originality as well as subjectivity has rendered impossible that genre of art called 'the primitive'. Yet it would seem that the instinct to create remains intact, part and parcel of the human spirit. Children can still draw and make clay figures. Those who have not been instructed can create. Creation as such is not and cannot be a global enterprise; artistic excellence will always manifest itself individually and specifically that is to say in an artist through a work. Originality, which is both subjective and objective, remains rooted in a particular situation, a specific moment, time and place, a concrete instance, standing apart from the world's passing fancy, declaring something new and yet partaking of the past. An integrity of relationship between artist and work is the necessary pre-requisite to this kind of originality, the responsibility for which will always lie with the artist, eschewing the attractive and the acceptable solutions proffered by artistic society in order that he or she may maintain that innocence of vision which sees beyond the present moment.

Art and Death

Two Contrasting Images of Death: or Horizontal and Vertical Images of Death

My death is certain but the hour is unsure,
Life is so brief and little now have I;
So sweet it is to sense, yet cannot lure
The soul. My spirit prays that I may die...

Oh God, when will that time arrive which he,
Who trusts in you, expects? Hope falls away,
And fatal to the soul is great delay...
Michelangelo *Sonnet* LXIX

NEARLY 75 YEARS SEPARATE Andrea Mantegna's *Il Cristo Morto* and the *Rondanini Pietà* of Michelangelo. The Mantegna painting's date of execution seems to be something of a matter for conjecture: a span of 15 years exists between the earliest possible date and the last. One thing is unquestioned however; it was created in the latter years of the artist's output. By contrast it is known with certainty that Michelangelo worked on his last *pietà* up until six days before his death. It remained unfinished, left in his studio, apparently bequeathed to his servant. The dead body of Christ is the central focus of both the Mantegna and the Michelangelo, but in many other ways the works are completely different: one is a painting, the other a sculpture; one finished, the other unfinished; one dealing with the finality of death, the other described by some as symbolic of the Resurrection.

The two works are located in Milan, a city which never approached the artistic productivity so evident in Renaissance Florence. Their siting is a fact of history, but the location is also important in so far as it affects how the works are presented and how the viewer sees them. I hesitate in using the word 'viewer', because the physical situation of neither of these works is comparable to that of a large metropolitan museum. One does not go from gallery to gallery, from painting to painting as for example in the Louvre or the Uffizi. One goes rather almost in the spirit of a pilgrimage, a lonely quiet encounter, which would be impossible in a large crowded museum gallery. The two works have an air of 'privacy' about them, given in part by their surroundings. They are to be seen, but are not 'on display' so to speak. In one sense they have no public 'persona' as do the first *pietà* of Michelangelo or Mantegna's great work for the Camera degli Sposi at Mantua. Both works are profoundly religious in character. By this I do not mean that they cannot be appreciated on a purely artistic plane, but rather to do so would be to fail to grasp the whole point of their existence. They speak about death, which unless it is understood as being of religious significance, is totally misunderstood. I realise these words may seem to some provocative or to others demonstrative of a narrow point of view, but what I mean is this. if death is only the final end of everything that pertains to the individual, merely the stopping point of so many 'one offs' or individuals, then it is of no significance; there is nothing to be feared or hoped for, precisely because there is nothing beyond (unless ironically one fears extinction). But if death, and its treatment by art, concerns the conclusion of earthly life (its closure and completion) then the eternal worth of that life and its 'depiction' by art must have a religious quality about it ie it must pertain to the eternal, therefore divine, and not the mere termination of temporal existence as we know it. Clearly this becomes even truer when the subject matter of the work of art is the dead Christ, even though one could argue that the vast number of art works of this period were concerned with a specifically religious subject matter. What I hope to reflect on in this paper is how the approach of death occasioned a radical shift in the formal expression the artists took in depicting it.

Some historical background is of importance here: both the works we are referring to were found in the respective artist's studios at the time of their death. They seem not to have been commissioned works. Concerning Michelangelo's this is almost certainly true. It was bequeathed to his servant Antonio del Francese, a fact which seems to express further the personal character of the work. Mantegna's painting and Michelangelo's sculpture, being latter works of the artist's lives, figure among several others which also deal with death: two *pietàs* (paintings) and the martyrdom of St Sebastian in the case of Mantegna, and several crucifixion drawings in the case of Michelangelo. The *Pietà of the Stone Cutters* by Mantegna is roughly of the same period as his *Il Cristo Morto* and is interesting in that, although it depicts a Madonna and Child, the Christchild instead of being portrayed in the customary sitting position is in a reclining position as for a *pietà*. The thought of death in this painting is further emphasised by the stony background reminiscent of scenes of Calvary. Mantegna's *Martyrdom of St Sebastian*, is also roughly of the same period, ie 1490, and bears the inscription: '*Nihil nisi divinum stabile est. Coetera fumus*' ('Nothing except the divine is stable. The rest is smoke'). St Sebastian stands framed in stone within a black background, of what can only have the semblance of a tomb. However vertical the depiction, the saint remains encased in a sepulcher, the only signs of life being the expression on the saint's face and his foot extending beyond the frame of the picture. Like the *Il Cristo Morto*, it too was found in the artist's studio at the time of his death and reflects the same theme.

The *Il Cristo Morto*, although not entirely surrounded by a frame of stone as is the *St Sebastian*, lies on a mortuary plinth. Its lighting has been described as having an air of 'eerie twilight'. Yet it is the body itself which diffuses the light in what is a strikingly limited pictorial space. From whatever vantage point one stands in this relatively small room, the figure of Christ commands our attention, not by following us, as some have suggested, but by drawing our eyes to the body placed on the wall. However, what remains the most impressive feature of the painting is its utterly bleak statement of death – death framed, motionless, final, incontestable. Yet in spite of this, an atmosphere of peace and stillness pervades. The grieving figures of the Virgin and St John almost seem to disturb this peace by their living presence (they are thought by some to be an addition and not by Mantegna himself). The figure of Christ is of another world, yet so defiantly present in this one. Such is the reality of the corpse: immoveable, but somehow absent. The entire plane of the picture is taken up by the body of the dead Christ. The mourners squeezed in to the left of the figure (from the viewer's perspective) only emphasise the magnitude of this death, where the mourners seem to be only of secondary importance. I can think of no other portrait of death in the history of art which portrays death so authentically. The word 'authentic' is important here, as signifying the entire 'feel' of death, rather than a merely accurate description of it. Here there is no expectation of the Resurrection. This is death alone, when the soul has gone, but and this is important: it remains the death of Christ in his humanity.

Michelangelo's *Rondanini Pietà* presents us with another view of death. The last work of an extraordinarily prolific career, it is Michelangelo's final statement. The *Rondanini Pietà* is often interpreted in a way similar to all the other *pietàs* created by the artist, including the *Florentine Pietà* with which it is sometimes linked. The two works are actually quite different. The *Florentine Pietà* was referred to both by Condivi and Vasari (biographers of Michelangelo) as a 'deposition' – a taking down of the dead body of Christ from the cross. The *Rondanini Pietà*, to which Condivi makes no reference (an uncommissioned work, begun in solitude and the artist's last expression), was perhaps begun as an entombment, as indicated by a group of studies, where Christ is being carried to the tomb by Mary and Joseph of Arimathea. But what was begun as an 'entombment' sculpture of three figures became in the end a standing *pietà* of two fused figures: the dead Christ and his Mother. As a whole it is unfinished but with finished parts: an arm that is separated from the whole and the completed legs of Christ, and hence it is a juxtaposition of finished and unfinished. Yet in spite of this there is a perfect balance of unity and movement. Spiritually the dominant theme is one of unity and support. The *Rondanini Pietà* as a *pietà* depicts the dead Christ and his Mother, but because it is a *pietà* it has always been assumed that the Virgin Mother would support the dead body of her Son. But visually, because the *Rondanini Pietà* has been 're-worked' on a vertical plane, and because the Mother stands behind her Son, the appearance is rather that of Christ supporting his Mother. In the Son's death their roles have been reversed. Christ in his death has become the living force supporting the dead weight of his grieving Mother. The frontal position of the figure of Christ in relation to his Mother, who stands behind her Son, perched as it were on his shoulders, gives the impression that he now has become the cross and she the victim. It is precisely in this reversal of roles that Michelangelo has created one of the most powerful images of redemption in the history of art. In dying, Christ gives life. In taking humanity upon himself quite literally in this image where he carries his Mother upon his shoulders, he bears all of humanity as he does his Mother. This posture of bearing, this gesture of carrying, is reminiscent of the earliest artistic Christian images of the 'Good Shepherd' found in the Roman catacombs. What is described as a *pietà* is as much an image of Redemption and Resurrection. Through the upward thrust of the figures it does in fact resemble more closely the numerous drawings of the Resurrection made by Michelangelo than it does any of the *pietàs* executed by him. In what can only be described as a profoundly Christian image, death gives birth to life. Unlike the Mantegna, whose arresting imagery is dependent on the foreshortened figure of the dead Christ lying in a completely prone position, and so forsaking the standard pictorial plane, it has become an image embedded in the wall rather than on the wall. By contrast in the *Rondanini Pietà*, Michelangelo has radically altered the normal configuration of a seated and reclining figure of Mother and Son to present a totally vertical composition, where the Mother no longer supports the body of her Son, but is rather supported by him. It is not a death which is being mourned, but a life which is being engendered, in this the artist's final work. It is a movement towards eternity, an unfinished gesture moving towards another place and a future time. And yet it is a finished work resolved in peace and rest.

Both Mantegna's *Il Cristo Morto* and Michelangelo's *Rondanini Pietà* were created at the time of life when death is no longer distant, and in the case of Michelangelo, when it was actually imminent. Is it this fact which is responsible for the radical change in their respective depictions of death and the extraordinary originality with which they expressed it? Is it their own death which they see in the image of the dead Christ, so that it is no longer merely the portrayal of an historical and biblical event, commissioned for a sacred building or executed as the result of a papal command but their very own death which they confront in the death of Christ? The fact that neither the painting nor the sculpture were commissioned and that they were found amongst the artists' last belongings are indications of their personal character. Rooted in the past, yet expressing something new and unknown, they denote the proximity of death, which has given birth to these final artistic testimonies.

How then do Mantegna and Michelangelo look at death? Mantegna has created a quasi-3D painting, totally horizontal in aspect, and yet it remains a two-dimensional painting affixed to a wall. Death has been literally 'walled in', an emphatic termination of life. The dull light, the utter stillness seems without hope. There is no life (it is interesting that the very last paintings Mantegna did were monochromes of classic themes, stone-like friezes (they have been described as 'sacred marbles')). The *Il Cristo Morto* presents death in its finality. Michelangelo's *Rondanini Pietà* on the other hand is totally vertical in movement, in contrast to the customarily seated *pietà* of the past. It is an unfinished piece, which fact allows, so to speak, a visual continuation. It is a figure of death in its movement towards life. The thrust of this last of Michelangelo's *pietàs* is the same as to be found in his drawings of the death, not the death of finality expressed in the Mantegna *Il Cristo Morto*, but a death which will become resurrection and life, a death which is redemption, human and divine.

Art and Death: the Endless Search, the Enduring Present

ART: WHATEVER IS firmly placed, made of matter, existing in time; what we can see and touch. Death: what comes after temporal knowledge; what we cannot know. Are these two separate worlds or are they one? Is art, that which seems so present to us, really part of a world which is hidden from us? Does how we make art affect how we view death, and does death determine the art we make?

These seemingly different worlds are actually connected and are but one; that art's objective presence forms a bridge between the present and the future; and what art is able to express concerning our present life is essentially of the same nature as that which we will know after death. Both art and death are concerned with the present moment, not the moment which is about to pass away, but the moment or moments when we step outside of time instead of being governed by it. Those 'small' revelations which are given us in art are of the same nature as that final summation of these moments which will be revealed to us at the moment of death. Much of contemporary art, however, rather than being an attention to the present moment is instead a constant projection forward of the recent past, where the artist's expectation of fame and fortune creates a wall between himself and the work on which he is engaged. This 'wall', largely of the artist's own making, prevents him from interpreting the past and using it in the present and, as it were, moving towards the future. It is the result of an inattentiveness to the present moment.

The attentiveness to the given moment bears none of the hallmarks of the 'cutting edge' mentality. The latter, rather than showing an attentive awareness to the here and now, exhibits a grasping possessiveness, a making my own of something which precludes the essentially shared meaning natural to art. 'Cutting edge' art functions rather as a commodity does in the world of the consumer: 'newer and better'. But the very nature of art eschews these temporally restricted divisions. The 'visions' of art transcend time, whilst ever being firmly rooted in it. There is an innate connection between today's relativism, which rejects the possibility of absolute truth and beauty and makes everything a matter of subjective taste, and the contemporary artist who views artistic activity as an occasion to flaunt one's own personal whims and fancies, what Picasso called 'making a present of one's personality'.

But what has the present moment to do with death, which until it happens always lies ahead of us? Death is the conclusion, the completion, the only moment which has no subsequent, the moment when one is immersed in the present of eternity. At death there is a total and complete awareness of all that has preceded. This complete awareness which death opens to us, needs to be an instinctive attitude in the artist. In a sort of aesthetic paradox, the present moment is something from which the artist must abstract himself, in order to be present to it. The situation of the artist is like that of a child at play. Time does not exist – it continues and the play becomes everything. It is not that the artist any more than the child can stand still; it is just that he is not concerned with other things, in order that he can be alone with what he is doing. This is being present to the present moment, that state of being which death assures, but which seems so difficult to attain in our day to day routine existence. Death is the completion of life; it is not the end of life. It is the completion of all those individual acts, seemingly so disconnected but re-united in that final unending awareness, that moment the understanding of which constitutes the life of every human person. In death one sees beyond the accepted seeing to see something new made of the old. That is the seeing which is necessary to the poet and the artist. In this 'artistic seeing', the artist, the poet, must see anew, the familiar must become unfamiliar in order that it may be seen anew. The artist must be removed from the present moment in order to see it more clearly.

This seeing is a kind of abstraction, a being taken away, a purification of sorts; and so the need for solitude in art as well as in life. It is a time for silence, that is, visual silence. The visual world we live in has no silence, because it has no space. The artist has become merged with his environment to the detriment of both. Without this visual silence the artist cannot be present to himself nor to his work. The work of art requires both that he be present to himself and to the world. An artist's complete absorption either in himself or in the world can only breed neurosis and sickness, and much of what we witness today is precisely that, only in a kind of ironic inversion, contemporary art witnesses an artist's complete absorption in the world which becomes a projection of his own self. It is a lack of solitude which produces this forcing of the world's image upon the artist so that he can only see himself, but as the world would have him be, so that he sees neither himself nor the world and so is unable to portray either. This diversion, distraction, or self-absorption ensures neither a presence to oneself nor to the world. The artist must isolate himself, at least psychologically from the habitual, which is often the most fashionable view offered by the world, including the world of the museum curator and art critic. This separation from the world is not that of the morbid melancholic romantic, but a choice, even if an unconscious need, to be alone in order to see clearly and without distraction. But does the artist's self-imposed isolation really have anything to do with death, any consideration of which some might think to be both morbid and pathological? The isolation, ideally physical but not necessarily, if the artist is adept at screening out unwanted distractions, is actually a sign of artistic and spiritual health, a preparation. In death our isolation from the world will be complete, not the preparatory isolation necessary to the artist, nor one over which we have any control, but the complete separation which will enable us to have that vision of fullness, theologically referred to as the 'beatific vision'. This is not a heavenly fantasy any more than the artist's creative expression can be an expression disconnected from reality. Although much of what we see today is just this.

Each artistic creation is made from something old but has become something new; it has left behind the old even as it may have made use of it. This leaving behind and entering into something new is a kind of death, a death which is and must be personal. The end of the 20th and the beginning of the 21st century has seen much art which might be called 'personal', but 'personal' in this sense has less to do with the individual person then with the projection of a subjective response to an accepted artistic milieu. Death can only be personal; no one can accompany us in our death, for when we come to meet God, and I believe this is what happens at death, it is the life of each person whole and entire that God wishes to confront, a confrontation which is an awakening for the individual, but not for God. Judgement is awareness. The personal nature of death is foreshadowed in each artistic creation where the artist too must stand alone and give account for the judgements that he has made in his work. It is not always conscious accounting, and in some senses it must not be. Art is not a matter of control, but it is something for which the artist himself is totally responsible; he cannot defer responsibility to someone outside of himself. His decisions can only come from himself, if they are to have any artistic integrity. To make what is wanted – art as commodity is not the same as to make what is required, and this latter is a totally personal choice.

How else is art like death? Death, which many identify with finality and end. Why does an artist continue to work if it is all to end anyway? Picasso said: 'The artist never finishes', and yet there are finished paintings. The artist like everyman seeks to know; he is never satisfied, but in a different way from the way others are not satisfied. Lack of satisfaction does not necessarily mean 'dissatisfaction' but it indicates a need, as it were, never to be finished. The artist must continue but he must not repeat himself (unless that repetition is to be part of the whole). Picasso noted that: 'Repetition is contrary to the laws of the spirit, to its flight forward'.[19] If the artist always continues to produce the same thing his work dies, not as death before new birth, a completion and fulfilment, but as an end. The artist is one who cannot end; he must always continue working – to go outside himself in order that he may return to himself. This is an act of purification – a redefinition for himself and for his work. A work of art is always related to what has preceded it, but it must never be static. It is always moving forward, longing, and mirroring the human soul itself. Rilke described the soul as 'only having an inkling of what it achieves, speaking to itself in riddles'.[20] The artist cannot have a completely conscious 'control' over his art; he often does not 'understand' what he does, even when he realises it is needful to what he is doing. The longing, characteristic of the artistic temperament (although this is often portrayed in a romantic and artificial way) 'wrests (man) from the contentment of everyday life... it wounds him and this very wound gives him wings drawing him upward... Beauty wounds but this is precisely how it awakens man to his ultimate destiny'. The longing, which the theologian Joseph Ratzinger speaks of as a 'wound' is ultimately only fulfilled in God and is often experienced by the artist as frustration – a feeling of never being satisfied. It is part of the human condition, but in the artist it is a necessary requisite. The contemporary artist Anselm Kiefer speaks of painting as of life as 'being a conglomeration of failings... (where) expectations are always unfulfilled'. But he also speaks of

---

[19] Dore Ashton, *Picasso on Art: A Selection of Views*, p.53.

[20] Rainer Maria Rilke, *Letters to a Young Poet*.

painting as 'a transformation which also transforms the artist'.[21] This transformation is the work of every individual. Its accomplishment can never be gauged in terms of success, for people are only successes and failures in terms of what is merely 'transitory', as Kiefer notes. The artist who seeks success no longer believes in the intrinsic truth and beauty of what he makes; he is concerned only with himself, and as an artist has failed. He has chosen the transitory and rejected the enduring.

The artist is often thought of as one who has the special ability to imitate (a significant word as it denotes something that is not real) and reproduce. He would be more accurately described as one who is able to see better or see differently. His restlessness, a part of his longing, the solitude he seems to require, his impatience with the routine, are the very things which allow the artist to see things afresh, to find the new hidden in the old. The understanding which every new work of art gives us is essentially an uncovering: it points to the future in that it is new, but is rooted in the past as being the uncovering of something which retains the vestiges of the familiar whilst transcending them. It belongs to the present; it is a bridge between the past and the future: 'the creation of a new relationship with the world, defining as such a real proximity to the world; (yet) it thrives in existential isolation, supposing a withdrawal from the world as fundamental as it is unique, a separation nowhere else attained'. But the 'uncovering' specific to death is in its totality so fundamental that it might seem to bear no relationship to the unveilings experienced in art. Art moves between these two worlds, the one totally hidden and the other apparent, or so it would seem, but in reality it is the artist's task to see and translate into a physical expression what is hidden in the temporal world. Ladislaus Boros describes the artist as existing in a 'frontier' position, for art is both concrete and transcendent – the manifestation of man's soul

---

[21] *The Guardian.*

and body. Anselm Kiefer refers to painting as transformation – a movement across, through and beyond. Death is the culmination of many transformations. It is the final and lasting one made up of all the others. But death is not finality in the sense of end, of closure, an eternal halt. It is rather completion, fulfilment, a consummation, a coming together. In contrast to the contemporary conception of death, which sees only finality and termination, the 4th century AD Greek Patristic St Gregory of Nyssa saw death and indeed all of the spiritual life as perpetual progress. This 'progress' must be distinguished from the present day scientific, economic notion. It is a progress in delight, an essentially evaluative term signifying an ever-growing appreciation which never terminates. It is the delight of love, and being such can never denote the merely transitory. To describe this progress Gregory uses the word '*epectasis*' – a Greek term meaning 'tension' or 'expansion', that is something which retains contact with what has preceded but which moves forward. Gregory saw life and death as one, or rather the latter as a continuation of the former. Man's transcendent nature is by that very fact never satiated; every satisfaction is an encouragement to something beyond. The term '*eros*' normally associated with physical attraction and possession becomes in Gregory what one commentator calls 'a symbol of supra-rational attraction drawing the soul irresistibly towards God'. The more inaccessible God seems the more fervently is he sought. In a commentary on the *Canticle of Canticles*, speaking of the Bride seeking her Beloved, in what is a seemingly endless search, Gregory expresses an attitude which could be applied to the artist – likewise engaged in an endless search.

> Picasso: 'have you ever seen a finished picture... Woe to you the day it is said that you are finished! To finish a picture? What nonsense! To finish it means to be through with it, to kill it, to rid it of its soul, to give it a final blow: the most unfortunate one for the painter as well as for the picture.'

Gregory: 'The true satisfaction of the (bride's) desire consists in constantly going on in her quest and never ceasing in her ascent, seeing that every fulfilment of her desire generates a further desire for the Transcendent. Thus the veil of her despair is torn away and the bride realises she will always discover more and more of the incomprehensible and unhoped for beauty of her Spouse throughout eternity. Then she is torn by an even more urgent longing...' [22]

The great French patristic scholar Jean Danielou describes this movement of the soul as 'a yearning which fills the soul more fully than actual possession... (but this in turn) displaces the soul and forces it to centre itself on God in an act of total dispossession'.[23] Is this not the disposition which we should expect that art would effect in the artist? Instead, at this present moment the contemporary art scene features a 'retrospective' exhibition of the sexual forays and resulting sadness of one of Britain's no longer Young British Artists Tracey Emin, as well as that of her YBA contemporary Damien Hirst's £65 million sale at Sotheby's, significantly entitled *Beautiful in my Head Forever* (£65 million was the predicted sum for the sale, in the end Hirst broke the world record for an auction dedicated to one artist fetching £111 million). If art is connected with death as an enduring reality, as affirmed in this essay, what can exhibitions which clearly do not present themselves as having any interest in objective excellence, but rather as personal display, indicate for the future of art, for our attitudes *vis-à-vis* the most fundamental of all questions, that of death, and for the death of one who calls himself or herself an artist? If the artist himself is replacing his work, and such would seem to be the case, if a statement in the *Daily Telegraph* of 5 August 2008 can be used as an example, where the critic refers to one contemporary artist as having 'become (herself) her most successful

---

[22] Gregory of Nyssa, *Homilies on the Song of Songs*.

[23] Jean Danielou, *God and Us*, p.201.

work of art', then art in its traditional sense as necessarily being an object has lost all meaning. In fact, it no longer exists and has been supplanted by the cult of celebrity. The artist who no longer looks beyond himself has given up that essential search vital to art. But art continues to exist in spite of the spiritual blindness of those who call themselves artists, because the nature of art of itself is enduring, even if those who practise it are not. 'For the eye does not tire of seeing...' (Eccl.1: 8). Art abides even as it tells us what we do not yet know or in terms of the spirituality of Gregory of Nyssa: 'The soul of man moves ceaselessly upward always reviving its tension for its onward flight by means of the progress it has already realised... it does not slacken its tension by action but rather increases it.' Death is the consummation of this endless search even while never placing a limit on it and thus forever fulfilling it. Art sustains us with the hope that tells of things we do not yet know. It is part of the endless search enduring forever.

Architecture

'To Innovate With Tradition', the Aesthetic Spirituality of Dom Paul Bellot, Architect and Monk

DOM PAUL BELLOT, monk and architect, was known for his innovation in both material and architectural form. Constrained by a monastic economy in his use of brick, he discovered new formal possibilities, which rather than limiting his creative need, provided him with a strikingly original means of expression.

Dom Bellot began his architectural studies at the *Ecole des Beaux Arts* in Paris and completed them before entering the monastery of St Pierre of Solesmes, then in exile on the Isle of Wight. Like many a monk or nun who has left a career in the world for the monastic life, he probably believed that his architectural skills had been put behind him forever in order that with a single eye he might give himself entirely to his monastic vocation. Yet shortly after his entry into the monastery he was called on by Dom Delatte, the abbot of St Pierre, to take up once again his skills as an architect. In March 1906 he was sent to the Netherlands by his abbot to supervise the construction of another monastery of the Solesmes Congregation, the Benedictine monastery of Oosterhoot. Having accomplished this assignment swiftly on his return he was immediately given a task well suited to his artistic training, the design of the new Abbey of Our Lady of Quarr on the Isle of Wight, which was to serve as the centre of the Congregation until its return to France from exile.

Dom Bellot was totally unskilled in the use of the brick, which was 'dictated in deference to the local building practice'. His father Paul Emile Bellot, an '*architecte-verficateur*' (a type of surveyor for the City of Paris) was able to provide Bellot with the technical information necessary in the use of brick. Bellot submitted his working drawings for the monastery to his father in order that prints could be made for the contractor, M Bellot also informed his son of any errors in the construction drawings. Gradually Bellot gained confidence in his use of brick and overcame his initial misgivings concerning the use of what were the masonry principles with brick, this 'seemingly to the chagrin of the Isle of Wight bricklayers'. Furthermore the island bricklayers disliked using imported Belgian bricks which were harder than the local bricks as well as differing in size from the British equivalent. In spite of these difficulties the workmen accomplished their task with precision and care including the execution of the brick polychromy of the vaulting etc was the veritable work of an artisan. From henceforth Bellot was to develop his architectural skills in brick to such an extent that he became known as the builder of churches in brick.

Although Dom Bellot began to use brick as his principle building material, perhaps more through economic constraint and local possibilities, its use soon became an aesthetic choice which allowed for an unlimited liberty of expression. In his lectures delivered in Canada in his '*Propos d'un Batisseur du Bon Dieu*' ('Principles of God's Builder'), he emphasised the importance of the constraints, and even the ensuing benefits, imposed on the architect *vis-à-vis* monastic economy, site restrictions, local building regulations, the possibilities of the material itself, historical needs as dictated by the architectural environs of the building and its history etc. These were the 'givens' with which the architect must deal, but they must not be considered so much as obstacles to be overcome as sources of inspiration for the imagination. 'These are the laws which free us, the constraints which guide us, the rules which permit us to give the most scope to our talents'.[24] This idea is basically monastic in its spirit, where freedom could be said to function within a 'system'. Its parameters are determined by the definitive choice which is made at the moment of final profession. Yet there is a true and lasting liberty which is guarded by fidelity to the vows. Every decision made, be it aesthetic or other, has its determinants, a given situation within which our choices are formed. These determinants can be considered limiting or liberating. It is a question of one's attitude. This is true of the monk and of the artist. For Dom Bellot the choice of brick opened new horizons not offered by stone, most notably in the added dimension of colour, where the all-important element of light was determined no longer solely by positive or negative space, volume or its absence, but by the infinite variations of colour and surface, which could indicate solidity or transparency.

Acquiring architectural principles, being aware of the historical precedents of the site, knowing the character of the material, the building regulations, all of these demand the attention of the architect. If he is to succeed he can ignore none of them. Aligned to this, is the principle that order is the foundation of beauty. 'Beauty is founded on the perfection of a thing, where measure and order are of the first importance.'[25] In this Bellot followed St Thomas Aquinas who provided the theological foundation for his aesthetic: 'beauty consists in the correct proportion of things.'[26] Bellot continues: 'that which is beautiful has an order of itself, where the parts are in proportion, and each part is joined to another in a manner which is totally natural and forms a complete whole.'[27] This latter point of being a 'complete whole' – *un seul tout* – is important in so far as

---

[24] Dom Bellot, *Principles of God's Builder* p.49.

[25] Dom Bellot, *Principles of God's Builder* p.61.

[26] *Summa Theologie.*

[27] Dom Bellot, *Principles of God's Builder* p.61.

it indicates that the proportions are dictated from within. Aquinas gives three conditions which serve as the basis for this order and hence for beauty: 1.'integrity of perfection, 2. harmonious proportion 3. clarity or luminosity'.[28] These conditions allow for a certain 'ease' or naturalness. What is natural is not forced. What does not belong to the natural integrity of a work intrudes on its inherent balance. This is true no matter what the object. This law prevails where there is a traditional notion to the word 'aesthetic'. Hence it is that Bellot says: 'There are in fact a thousand ways to realise the notion of integrity of perfection or completion.'[29] What is believed to have been implied by the 'order of proportion' of which Aquinas speaks, and which deeply influenced the work of Bellot, was the unity created from diversity (something one thinks of as an inherently monastic virtue). 'The more there is a complete unity within the multiplicity the more striking is the proportion and the greater the beauty.'[30] Indeed one could say that the creative spirit requires a 'new' set of proportions suited to each new work. The integrity, the unity of the work, its ultimate success, is determined from within. 'Proportion changes with each work and according to the ultimate end... which is to say that every work poses a new problem.'[31] The diversity of the parts which form each work are reflected in the multiplicity of possibilities open to the artist and which he creates himself: 'every work produces a test for the creativity of the artist.'[32] In the achievement of each individual work the artist reflects the divine creativity. God alone creates singly. 'Beauty is concerned with singularity, we strive to imitate the Creator.'[33]

---

[28] As referenced in Dom Bellot, *Principles of God's Builder* p.62.

[29] Dom Bellot, *Principles of God's Builder* p.62.

[30] Ibid.

[31] Ibid, p.65.

[32] Ibid.

[33] Ibid.

Art in the traditional sense of the word must always have some principle of order within itself. This does not mean that a prescription of order can be given in advance, but that each work has within itself its own order or integrity, be this a work of art of minimalist description or a work of abstract expressionism. But architecture by definition operates on two different planes: practical and functional, as well as aesthetic. The 'beautiful' is not an addition to some basic formula of construction. 'Beauty is not something added to an object, but is fundamentally a part of it. The architect must know how best to profit from the laws of utility so that they are the source of the beauty that is derived from them.'[34] Dom Bellot at no time considered the technical requirements of his art as something tyrannical. They were to him an aid, the foundation on which he was to build.

Bellot's monastic training included a thorough knowledge of the theology of St Thomas Aquinas. The Thomistic aesthetic principles with which he was imbued were made clear in the lectures which he gave in Canada towards the end of his life and in the concluding years of WWII. In them he speaks of the *unique necessaire,* a single-minded focus on God which dictated the spirit with which everything must be done, a zeal for the Lord's House and His Glory. This zeal precluded anything tepid or reluctant and committed the monk to a constant battle, one of self – renunciation and self-mastery. This was no less so for Bellot the architect than for Bellot the monk. The monastic discipline penetrated his work as an artist. It was not enough to be well informed, well equipped, having to hand all the technical requirements necessary to accomplish the task:

> First of all one had to be on the offensive against our natural laziness to do that which is easiest. One must avoid habits, and take up positions which are the opposite of those established after many years. One had to establish at all costs silence and peace.

---

[34] Dom Bellot, *Principles of God's Builder* p.68.

> Silence and peace come from within. They take their strength from the will. One's labour has to be calm and peaceful, surrounded by reflection and prayer. Of course one had to have a technical foundation, which is an indispensable condition, but technique without energy is sterile, and faith is the best source of energy. It is a great pity in the domain of religious architecture when one seems to consider in his heart the sublimity of his work *vis-à-vis* its importance in the realm of faith.[35]

The whole of Dom Bellot's architectural work must be seen as an expression of his fidelity to the monastic spirit. The fact that he was thoroughly a monk in no way precluded the realisation of his artistic talents. Instead his basic monastic discipline was the source and foundation of all his inspiration. As a monk he was God's workman before all else. This fact allowed him to understand the monastic building from within. Each practical need had its spiritual counterpart.

'Being essentially a parable, the work of art does not have as its end the imitation of nature, but rather using the things of nature to advance the dialogue between the soul and God and God and the soul.'[36] All that the monk does is done within this spiritual realm, be it art or any other activity. In his artistic work a monk furthers the divine creativity, and grows in his awareness of God. But this is not a singular and exclusive relationship, but one which benefits the monastery and community as a whole as well as the world beyond. And when it is the case of an architect of Bellot's calibre, what remains is a historical testimony to the good and the beautiful, something which is handed on.

Etymologically 'tradition' comes from the Latin word *tradere*. It means to hand over; it assumes an ongoing movement. It presumes

---

[35] Dom Bellot, *Principles of God's Builder* p.68-69.

[36] Ibid, p.71.

a past but it does not rest there. The artist, the architect, does not exist in isolation. He exists at a particular time and in a particular place. He is part of a tradition, whether he is conscious of it or not. Being part of a tradition does not mean replicating the past. It does not, as Bellot says in his 'propos' consist in 'resurrecting a cadaver. The art of the past is of the past'.[37] Neither is it a case of making 'slavish copies'.[38] 'To innovate with tradition' is neither reproducing the past nor rejecting it. Rather it is: *vetera novis augere*, 'enriching the old with the new'. What is possible to the artist does to a certain extent depend on what has gone before, even if it is in order that it be rejected. To judge, to choose, is to select even when this means discarding. One must learn from the past in order to advance, this is so, as much for the artist as it is for the monk. It is not a question of a slavish imitation but of a judicious selection according to the principle of fidelity to a purpose. The integrity and clarity which Dom Bellot demonstrated in his work as an architect were likewise reflected in his life as a monk. Each could be said to have enriched the other.

------

[37] Dom Bellot, *Principles of God's Builder* p.53.
[38] Dom Bellot, *Principles of God's Builder* p.5.

Visual Silence in Monastic Architecture: Cistercian Architecture of the 12th and 13th Centuries

THE RULE OF ST BENEDICT prescribes silence at numerous times and in numerous places. It is a manner of behaviour that the monk or nun must learn to acquire if he or she is to persist in his monastic calling. It both teaches constancy in the monastic life and is a tool necessary to the acquisition of humility and obedience and the practice of charity in the community. It is a *habitus* acquired through will and desire, but its expression is to be found not only in the practice of monastic decorum, but also in the material ambience which is customary to monasteries. No more was this so then in the Cistercian monasteries of the Middle Ages, where the simplicity of expression was to be seen in every architectural detail as well as in the co-ordination of the geographical site, the use of materials, and in the working out of the economic needs and possibilities of the community. This fundamental *necessarium* – silence – had its physical correlate in separation from the world. This was a further manifestation of the the silence that the Holy Rule sets down as necessary to the monk or nun's personal relationship with God.

Monasticism as the word indicates is focussed on a single thing, a single One. If this is so it must be free from distraction, from that which leads the monk or nun away from this single pursuit. Distractions are as many and varied as the human imagination, but they can be neutral in so far as they are not self-generated but come from the surrounding background, but they are not for that any less distracting. They are audibly or visually distracting, interfering with the focus of one's attention.

Every monastery is particular; its peace is particular. It is what the monk or nun will find on first arriving and it will remain with him all his life. It will become part of him and he of it. There are however certain principles or similarities that can be found in the monastic place which contribute to this peace. This peace is not pursued by a single individual but in the company of others. Hence there are rules and regulations, 'customs' which are followed in order that this peace may be available to all. But as with all things there are physical places and settings, 'ambiences' which are more conducive to peace and silence – a quiet room, a quiet place. The monastic church is above all the place of peace and silence; it is the place of prayer. Hence it is we see that in the Cistercian churches of the 10th and 11th centuries there is a pronounced emphasis on simplicity, yet this simplicity was not so much 'barren' or 'empty' as balanced and measured, not by a soulless calculation but in an equitable peace through the use of light and dark, line and form. Based on the general principles set out in his *Apologia* to William of St Thierry, St Bernard derides anything that would distract the monk from his quest for God in prayer through superfluous decoration: 'For the sake of Christ we have abandoned all the world holds valuable and attractive. All that is beautiful in sight and sound and scent we have left behind, all that is pleasant to taste and tough.'[39] The Church was to epitomise that peace necessary to prayer, but its order and simplicity was to be found throughout the monastery as a whole, where a harmony of function and order was to reign down to the last detail eg the site of the monastery, the use of water in all its many forms, the need for light, heating, ventilation etc. The monk's life was oriented towards God, but all was done in communion with

---

[39] Bernard of Clairvaux, *Apologia ad Guillelmum*.

others. Of course building a monastery was a physical activity, and, contrary to what is often supposed, it was often done by Master builders and stone masons for the simple reason that the monks were engaged daily and hourly in that activity which was particular to the monk: the Opus Dei. However the conception and building of a monastery was a 'contemplative activity'. Contemplation, the need for silence, determined the quality of the building, what St Thomas Aquinas might have called the connaturality between prayer and its physical expression, an ambience of silence, a lack of fussiness, a simplicity of line and form, the use or lack of light to still the movements of the heart. St Benedict himself was quite precise about the need for silence in the oratory, and this silence seems to refer not just to the absence of speech, but also to a lack of clutter; nothing that does not pertain to prayer was to be kept in the oratory. St Bernard was to carry these prescriptions further indicating what might constitute a visual infringement of the rule of silence. What was suitable for the laity (the use of colour and images) was not suitable for the monk who was devoted to contemplation... for the soul must first transcend every material reality and every corporeal image before it could attain union with the absolute spirituality of God. This was a frequent theme in St Bernard's Sermons where he refers to the 'restless intrusion of sensible images' that disturb the rest of the soul in God. So-called 'monastic' art should not interfere with 'the discipline of the eyes' necessary to the practice of contemplation.

Monastic art or the art appropriate to monasteries was not so much the presence of art as an orderliness of simplicity which betokens that silence necessary to prayer. The early Cistercians were the craftsmen par excellence of this form of art. It was a disciplined art which benefited the community within which it was practised; it in no way reflected back on the practitioner but made the monastic life possible with all its exacting and specialised needs, those of seclusion and quiet, where God could be praised and the monk could attend to the needs of his brethren and his own unique relationship with the Lord.

Just as St Benedict, following the Gospel, prescribed that prayer should be made in few words St Bernard recommended that in the oratory there should not be many distractions, what one could call the 'visually discursive elements' leading the monk or nun away from the simple business of prayer. What in the Holy Rule is basically an audio prescription: '*non in clamosa voce... sed in intentione cordis*' becomes in St Bernard a visual prescription 'not in many images '. Images based on the biblical narratives of the Gospel were the basis for the great Cathedral churches but also of many other churches frequented by the faithful, but that which was necessary for the teaching of the faithful, were not in Bernard's view suitable in a monastic church for monks whose needs were 'spiritual' rather than 'carnal'. Bernard seems to oppose the visually didactic means of narration to the spiritual and contemplative use of the Word of God throughout the liturgical year. What Bernard seems to indicate as a suitable ambience for prayer is one devoid of image, for images distract (L. '*dis-trahere*') from God rather than centring on Him... the church must be simple and ordered, but in this most basic prescription the focus comes in the activity of prayer and is not provided from without. Silence and quiet, a natural light, which passes with the day, are the setting for the monk's prayer. In prayer the monk is drawn towards God, his intention is centred here, that ambience which allows for prayer and does not determine it.

Although there is no exact prescription for a monastic church, there are distinctive features that are found in the early Cistercian churches. These are notably: simplicity, harmony, balance, the importance of the use of light, and the absence of the use of colour. The first three would seem to be concerned with the 3D and the latter two the two dimensional, but in fact the use of light the absence of colour are a significant part of the 3D notions of simplicity, harmony and balance. For the use of light is essential in delineating mass and its balance; and absence of colour allows matter to speak on its own terms as a solid form. Light is for St Bernard an important symbolic notion which appears in many of his writings and denotes the divine light which is Christ, but is perhaps more difficult to explain or describe its presence in Cistercian architecture of this period. Light has no solidity, but neither is it mere space, for space can be full of light or full of darkness. Light is not absence; it is what one could call the fullness of space. Light is essential that all else may be seen, but an excess of it can be equivalent to its total absence. Cistercian architecture was dependent on the light of nature. The character of each building would change with the season of year. Each season had its own particular light and each part of the monastery would become different as the seasons changed. The stone according to its character would likewise modulate with the light, being flat or round, having depth or being shallow, and the lines of each mass would acquire depth with the passing of the sun. The lack of colour gave an eloquence to the stone; its 3-dimensionality became more substantial, its surface qualities more apparent. There was no room for anything artificial or 'painted on', each area became an 'habitus' and had a character of its own. As such, each silent space confirmed the general character of the monastery as a whole.

What was the secret of this 'visual silence'? A constraint of visual possibilities, an intentional sobriety dependent on the possibilities of nature and economy, but including these, an emphasis on the richness that nature herself provided, a rigorous adhesion to simplicity and order, not merely and only to prevent distraction but to allow for a unity in the monastic surroundings which had as its foundation a unity of persons with a single occupation, the adoration and contemplation of God, a single activity, the engagement in required the unified support of body and soul. St Benedict, the father of moderation and discretion knew the needs of the body and the soul. St Bernard was to realise these needs in a perfected harmony whose beauty was not to be surpassed in a silent and yet eloquent statement of architectural integrity.

APPENDIX

THE ESSAYS WHICH form this book vary in theme for the reasons I have noted above, but they also follow the development of my academic and artistic training, which began with philosophy, moved into a more specific interest in the aesthetic, and the belief that the aesthetic dimension in life often bears the closest connection to the notion of truth. The true and the beautiful are intimately linked with one another, and frequently one comes to the truth through the beautiful. It could be said that the clearest expression of the truth is in the beautiful. The beautiful explains itself; it does not need interpretation. Eventually my philosophical studies, with their emphasis on the aesthetic dimension sought a 'verification' in artistic form. I came to choose sculpture as the form which was most accessible to me and gradually, after entering the monastery, my interest in sculpture became translated into a more functional form: the making of furniture and garden structures, and eventually this came to take on an architectural way of seeing plants and trees as being bearers of form and colour. The various works in the book are always seen in situ and one of the last works 'the Garth Retreat garden' is given as an aperçu of a little corner of quiet retreat. We have provided a map of the plants, so that those interested can get an idea of size and scale, shape and colour.

My work appeared, as did the essays in this book, over a long span of time. Although I might be able to indicate what the source of inspiration was for some of the works this is by no means true for all of the works, for example Fald Stool (this chair is based on a 'Fald Stool', but why I decided to do that I don't know). These are artistic works and one cannot nor should, I think, want to trace the evolution of each work. That is a verbal process, not an artistic process. To try and give reasons for artistic works is, to a certain extent, to call into question the raison-d'etre of the work as artwork ie 'tell me what this means'. The captions which I give under each photo are as much detail as I am able to provide.

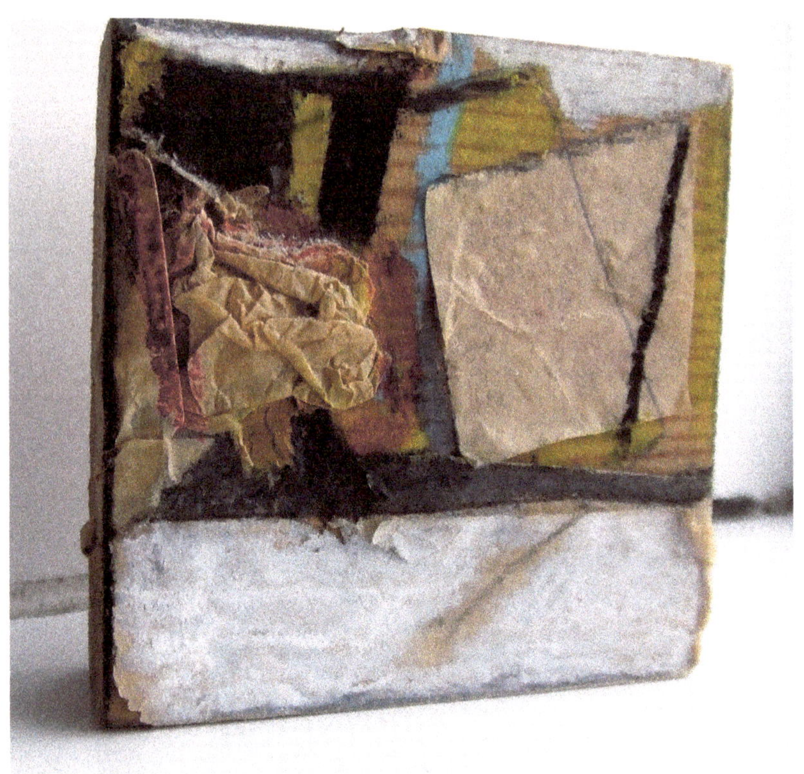

Schwitters in Miniature. I have always admired Kurt Schwitters and his ability use 'stuff', 'junk', as artistic stuff and compose a 3-dimensional piece of art in a very convincing manner.

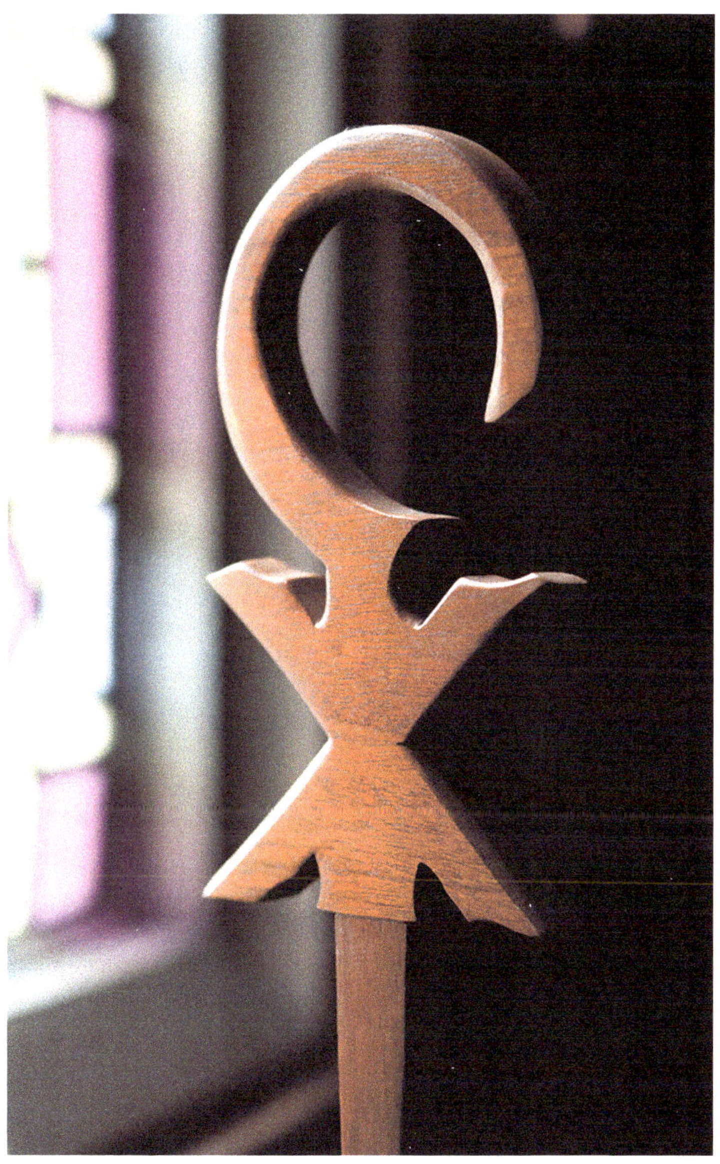

Crozier. Made for my Abbess. It is a symbol of her pastoral authority, which she carries on important feast days in the liturgical year.

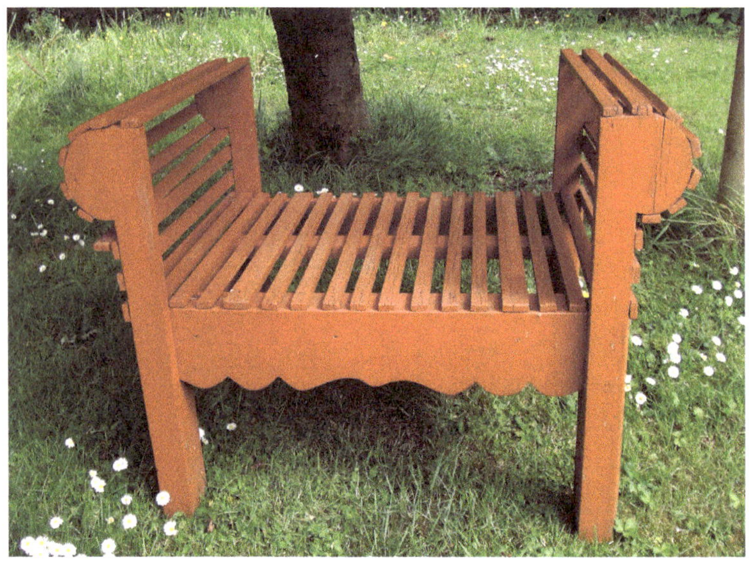

Mutti's Chair. 'Mutti' is an affectionate name for Mother Abbess, for whom I made the chair.

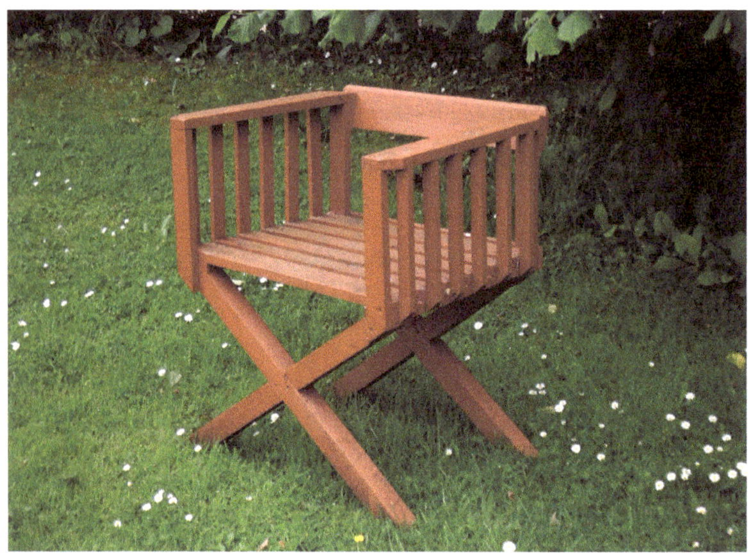

Fald Stool. A type of chair used in a liturgical setting.

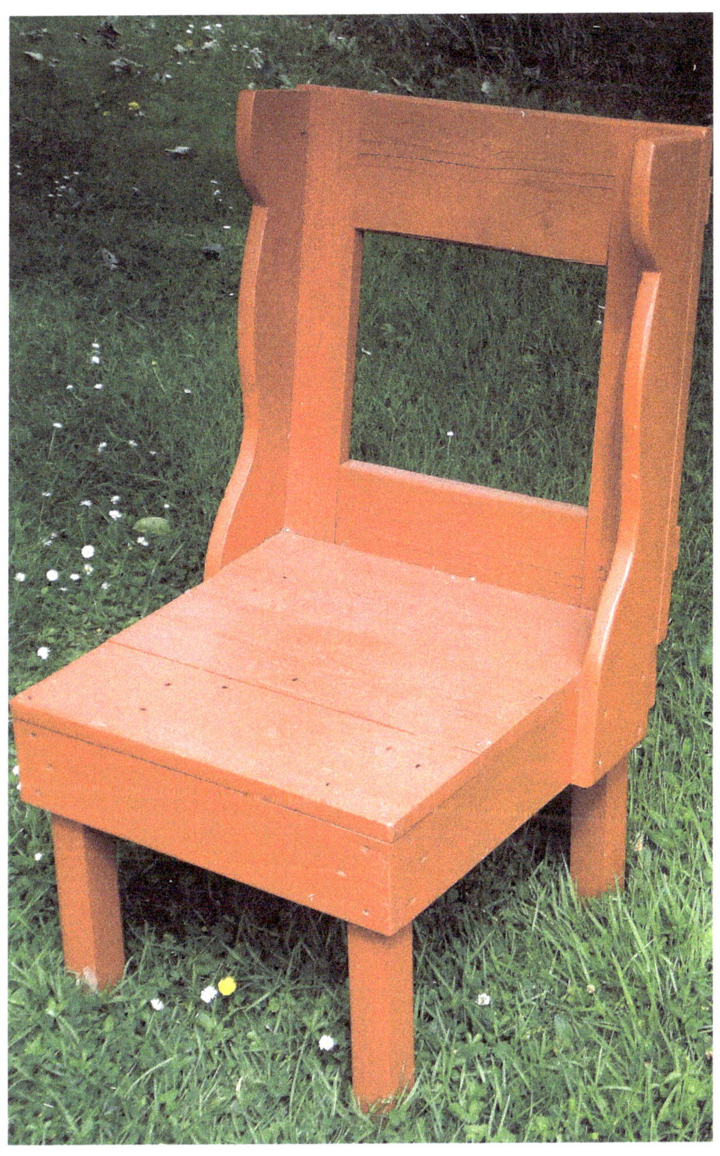

Matisse Chair, in so far as the shapes of the chair are reminiscent of
Henri Matisse's cut out collages.

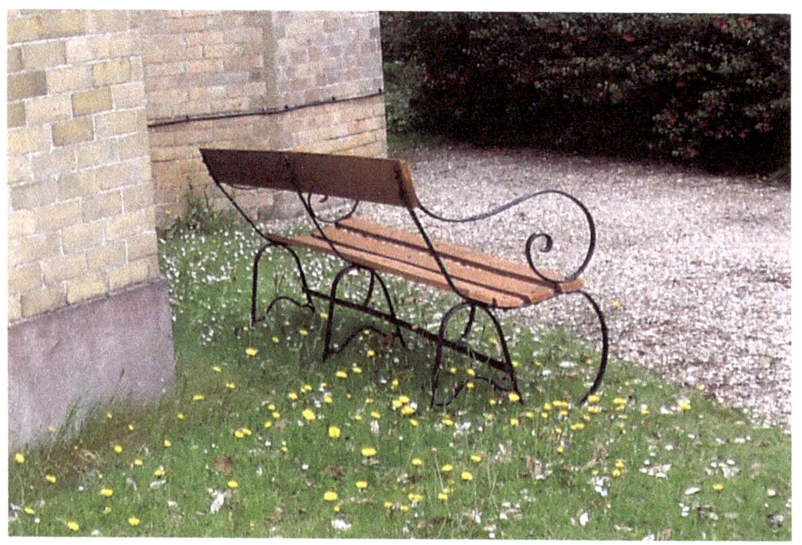

Iron Bench, based on a similar Victorian Bench originally found in our garden.

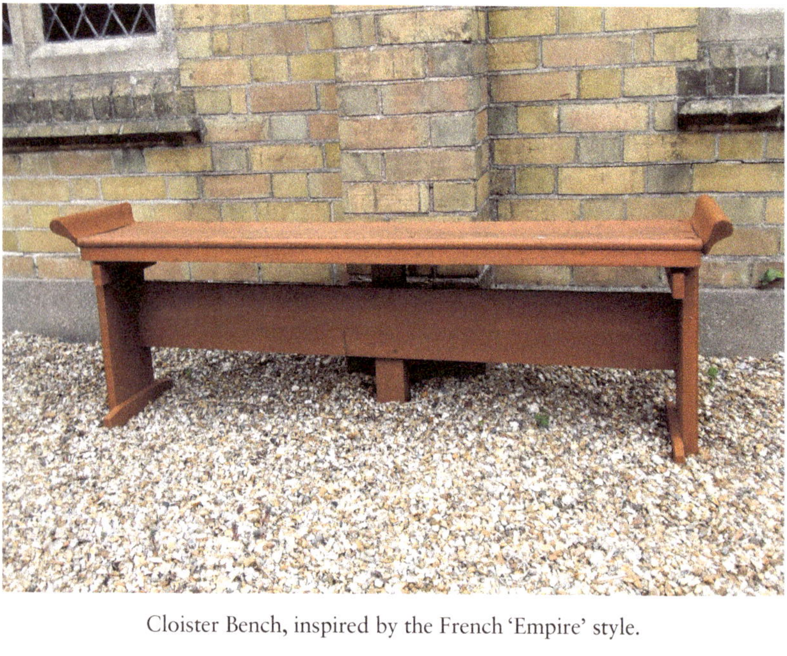

Cloister Bench, inspired by the French 'Empire' style.

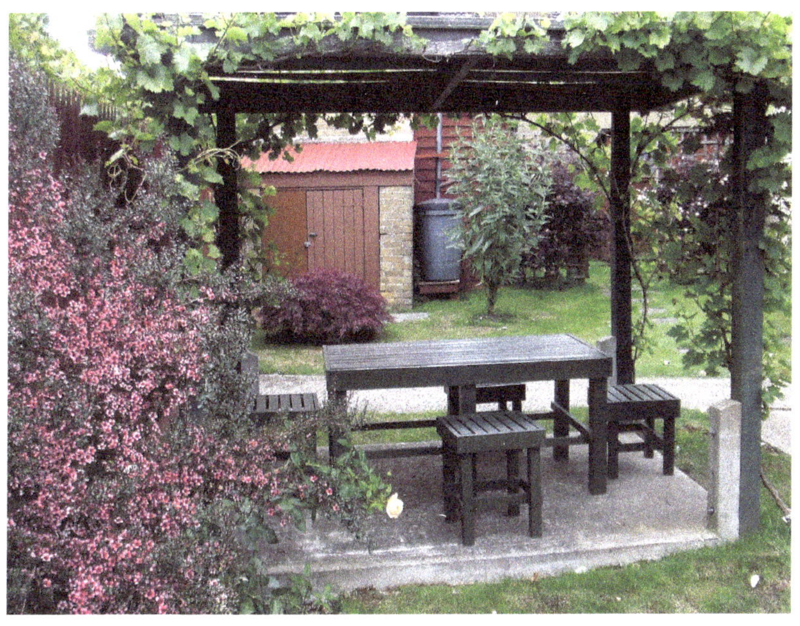

Arbour, Table and Stools. The central focus of our Garth Retreat Garden.

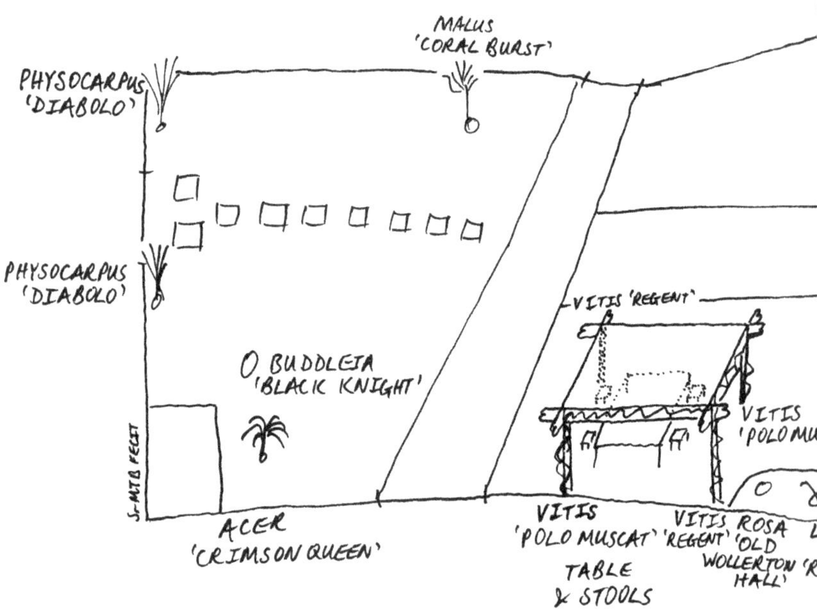

Garden map. Credit: Sister M Thomas

HOLLY

HYDRANGEA
SERRATA

MALUS
PENDULANS
'LOUISA'

BERBERUS
'ROSE GLOW'

CEANOTHUS
'CONCHA'

BERBERUS
'ROSE GLOW'

BERBERUS
'ROSE GLOW'

CHAIRS

BENCH

ROSA
'TRANQUILITY'

ROSA
'L. D.
BRAITHWAITE'

BUDDLEIA
VARIEGATA

ACER
BRILLIAN-
TISSIMUM

ROSA
'GRAHAM
THOMAS'

VIBURNUM
BODNAMTENSE

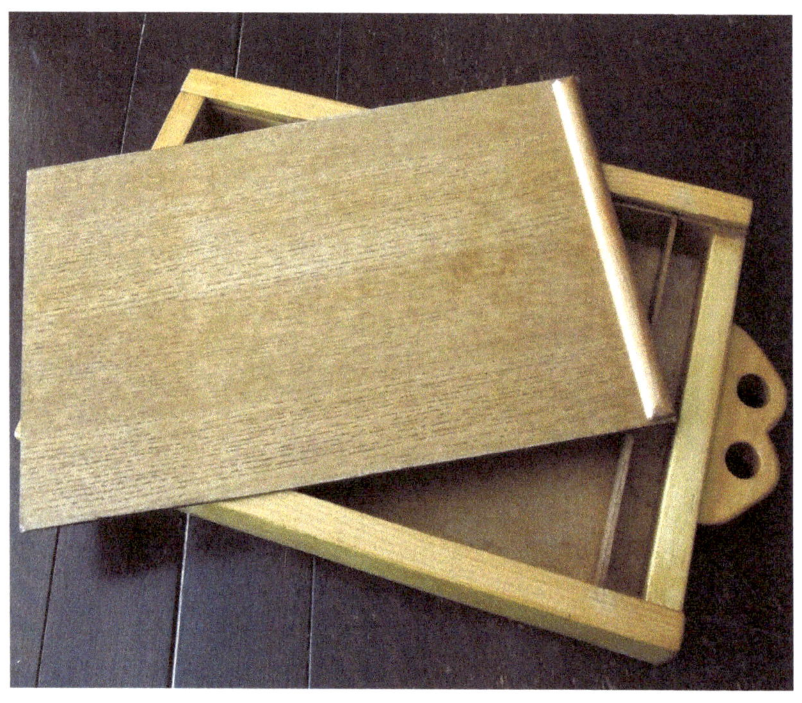

Writing Case: a case I designed and made for 'Correspondence Sunday' so that sisters who prefer to go outside to write their letters can carry their paper and writing tools to the garden with them.